MW01097912

HERE'S WHAT THE EXPERTS ARE SAYING
ABOUT THE BOOK VOLLEYBALL CYBERNETICS:

"Because volleyball has become a mind game, the fabulous insights in this book can improve the performance of any player at any level."

Leonid Yelin, 1995 Division II Coach of the year, Barry University (National Champions), Currently Head Women's coach, University of Louisville

"I've always believed in the adage, 'If you can believe it, you can achieve it.' As a coach I am always looking for a better way to explain this attitutde to my players and now I have one in 'Volleyball Cybernetics.' This is must reading for coach and player alike."

Bill Walton, Head Women's Coach, University of Houston

"Thoroughly intriguing. Using this book as a basis, now I can properly train our players in the psychological aspects for optimal performance."

Rich Luenemann, Head Women's Coach, College of St. Francis – NAIA Hall of Fame

"Without question, the most logical and clear work in training the mind for full playing potential. We could not have stayed focused through our 41-0 record and a state high school championship without the methods of Volleyball Cybernetics."

Dave Deuser, Head Men's Coach, Lewis University, Illinois – 1996 National Final Four

"Having coached for fourteen years makes me wish this book had been out fifteen years ago. Easy to read and highly motivational, Volleyball Cybernetics makes playing this game fun."

Marty Petersen, Head Women's Coach, University of Wisconsin-Oshkosh
1996 Asics/VOLLEYBALL NCAA Division III Coach of the Year

"Since being introduced to the Volleyball Cybernetics mental training program, our team has used the visualization and relaxation methods before every match. These and other inner game techniques of Volleyball Cybernetics have definitely made a positive impact on our program."

Sue Subich, Head Coach, Mansfield Madison High School, Mansfield, Ohio
Division I Coach of the Year – 1994, '95

"Finally a practical book that addresses the most elusive aspect of coaching… the 'mind set'! There's nothing like it anywhere in our sport. I applaud the efforts of Stan and Dave and thank them for writing it."

Maxine Mehus, Head Women's Coach, Emporia State University, Kansas

"From worst to first! Volleyball Cybernetics played a big part in our program's turn around this past season. The game of volleyball is more mental than any other team sport. Read this book and you'll know how to handle pressure, develop that winning feeling, and if you're a coach, jump start your program… like it did mine."

Tom Hughes, Head Women's Coach, Kansas Wesleyan University, Kansas, Conference Champions 1996

"Your visualization techniques were especially useful in preparing me for the intensive pressure of game situations. They helped me to remain positive and focused during these stressful moments."

Kim Woodring, Two Time NCAA Division III All American (1995, '97), Wittenberg University

"Volleyball Cybernetics is a must read for every volleyball coach and athlete. Because our game is 90% mental, this book will truly help you become the winner you want to be."

Steve Dallman, Head Women's Coach, University of Southern Mississippi

"Some of our greatest individual and team improvements have been produced by the methods of Volleyball Cybernetics. If you're a coach or player who has ignored mental training, this is a great book to start."

Wick Colchagoff, Head Women's Coach, Nebraska Wesleyan University

"Immediately useful. I was so impressed by what I read, I wasted no time applying the methods with my team."

Marilyn McReavy Nolen, Head Women's Coach, Saint Louis University
Named as an All Time Great Coach by USA Volleyball – 1995

"When I ask most coaches what they need to be more successful the overwhelming answer is a team psychologist. Well, here's one in a book! The techniques explained here are easy to understand and apply for both coaches and players, and best of all, THEY WORK!"

Mike Gibson, Head Women's Coach, University of Michigan-Dearborn

Volleyball Cybernetics

STAN KELLNER
AND
DAVE CROSS

BASED ON THE NATIONALLY ACCLAIMED
"YES, I CAN!" VOLLEYBALL SUCCESS TRAINING PROGRAM

A "YES, I CAN!" Publication

First Printing: March, 1997
Second Printing: April, 1998
Third Printing: November, 1999

Published by
"Yes, I Can!" Publications
Long Island, New York

Parts of this book are available on video and audio cassettes.
To contact Stan or Dave:

Stan Kellner, P.O. Box 134, East Setauket, New York, 11733
Telephone: (516) 751-3513
Fax: (516) 751-3589
E-Mail: stan@yesicansports.com

Dave Cross, 365 North Abbe Rd., Elyria, Ohio, 44035
Telephone: (440) 365-3329   Fax: (440) 365-0321
Dave's Toll Free Phone: 1-877-220-5828
E-Mail: dave@yesicansports.com
Web: www.yesicansports.com

Typesetting and graphic services by
Spring Harvey Design
New York, New York

Cover design: John Decker
Emporia, Kansas
Cover photography: Robert Beck

Printing by
Edwards Brothers, Inc.
Ann Arbor, Michigan

Photography by Great Lakes Photography
and The Elyria Chronicle Telegram

Manufactured in the United States of America
ISBN 0-965 6175-0-5

This book is dedicated to the memory of my parents, Jacob and Cecilia, whose synergistic efforts made the writing of this book possible.

Stan Kellner

To the memory of my parents, Frank and Pauline, who taught me the power of perseverence.

"Although your journey along life's path has ended, your spirit will always live on in my heart."

Dave Cross

ACKNOWLEDGEMENTS

Many wonderful people have stepped into our lives to counsel and support the creation of this book. With heartfelt appreciation we would like to thank them.

First and foremost my wife, Martha, who illuminates my life with much love, patience, and intelligence. Her editorial touch is on every page of this book as well as on every project in my life.

Linda Chapin, Kris Wagers, Spring Harvey, John Decker. We are indebted to your remarkable talents. And to Tom Hughes, a long-time, true friend. Your contributions have enriched this book and the "Yes, I Can!" program.

-Stan Kellner

Back in the summer of 1986 I had the opportunity to work at a volleyball camp called "Yes, I Can!" in Ohio. Little did I know that this camp and the super group of people I would meet in connection with it, would have such a profound influence on my life. I would like to thank the following list of friends who have had a hand in the development of the concepts explained in these pages:

Joe Kolodka, my partner in Ohio since the beginning, whose influence can be found on every page of this book.

Mike Gibson, our program director and volleyball's "Master of Mentalness" who has given of himself so unselfishly in the development of our program and in the writing of this book.

Bill Immler, Stan's original Ohio connection, who gave me an opportunity when I most needed one.

Steve Dallman, Wick Colchagoff, Sue Subich, Ivan Fedorsuk, and Scott Blanchard –the core of our staff. Each has contributed greatly to the shaping of the "Yes, I Can!" program and to my own growth as a coach.

John Dziatlik (J.D.) and Dave Wilcyznski (Wil) –my assistants at Keystone during the "early years" who worked so diligently to help develop our program and give me a player's eye view.

All the young ladies who "pulled up the kneepads" since the fall of 1986 for the Keystone Wildcats. None of this would have happened without my association with a steady flow of hard working and dedicated athletes.

To the memory of The Richman Boys – Doug, the first to show me the strength of positive thinking, and Denny, my first assistant coach, who helped me discover my love of coaching.

And to the memory of Phil Pirman, whose encouragement and support were responsible for my start in volleyball.

-Dave Cross

An Important Note

Parts of this book are based on Stan Kellner's book
Beyond The Absolute Limit with Basketball Cybernetics.
The reader is assured that this book is pure volleyball.

TABLE OF CONTENTS

A WORD FROM THE AUTHORS

Do you have a volleyball dream, a fiery passion to be the best volleyball player you can be? We hope so; because without a commitment to excellence, this book is not for you.

However, if a funny thing happens to your performance on the way to match point, and you mess it up, and enough is enough; then this book is definitely a must read.

What's holding you back from being the volleyball player you want to be? Is it a lack of talent, poor coaching, catching the right breaks, some bad calls, or are you on the wrong team? If you're ready to trade these excuses for excellence and take personal responsibility for your playing destiny, then read on. We can help you live your volleyball dream.

You're about to discover an inside-out training process that's been around for over 25 years helping athletes get their game in high gear. The name of the success process is **Volleyball Cybernetics.** Because of it, you'll find a very reliable computer-like internal success system, the one that you've always had buried inside your head. The power mechanism of this goal-seeking system is your subconscious. Once you learn how to get it to work for you, rather than against you, some very happy coincidences will happen to your game on the volleyball court. You'll be in the right place at the right time, doing the right things.

So if you're ready to learn how easy it is to develop the winner's mind game, turn the page. Your life on the court may never again be the same. Life off the court may have a different look, too.

Introduction

THE GENIE WITHIN

Imagine walking the beach one day and finding a corked bottle washed up on the shore. Picture yourself removing the cork then watching in amazement as a magical genie with wish-granting ability suddenly pops out of the bottle. Appreciative of being released from the bondage of the bottle, the grateful genie exclaims, "Tell me your most desired wishes and they will be fulfilled!"

Try to imagine what life on the volleyball court would be like with the support of a friendly genie magically providing you with the winning skills, attitudes, and even the breaks of the game whenever needed. Awesome concept, isn't it? Think of it. You could have whatever you want, whenever you want it, just for the asking.

What's your desire as a volleyball player? Is it a quicker arm swing? More aggressiveness at the net? A more accurate and powerful serve? To block, set, and dig with the consistency of a Karch Karaly?

We have both good and bad news for you. First, the good stuff. The fact is there is a powerful, wish-granting genie in your life. No, you won't find it in a bottle; it's there inside your head, and we don't mean in your imagination, either. This friendly genie is located in the space between your ears, inside your brain. The genie has several names but let's refer to it by its more common name...**the subconscious.** Believe it or not, your subconscious actually has the power to provide you with the level of skills and attitudes (yes, even the breaks of the game) needed to play at the performance level you desire.

The subconscious is your habitmaker, responsible for remembering and producing all of those physical skills you don't have time to think about, but just do. From walking, talking, and chewing gum to all of your volleyball skills, the list is endless. How well you perform these automatic, non-thinking skills is also within the job description of your subconscious.

xv

Another of its primary life-serving functions is to creatively achieve goals that have been given to it by your conscious mind. Your subconscious is a creative genius. Give it a problem to solve or a task to perform, supply it with the right kind of commands, and this very reliable mechanism will do what it has been designed to do which is to serve your needs. A genie second to none.

Best of all — and this is essential to the training success of **Volleyball Cybernetics** — your subconscious works automatically on signals called feedback. Just like any man-made computer, your subconscious is cybernetic in nature. Cyber what?

The **Science of Cybernetics** initially accomplished the task of putting brains into all kinds of machines like the electronic computer. Even the thermostat automatically controlling the temperature in the room you're in now, operates cybernetically. Any machine that has been designed for a specific purpose and works on signals called feedback is cybernetic.

What's more, the science of "thinking machines" has helped us understand why and how the human brain and nervous system operate with such split second precision. You're going to use these insights from the **Science of Cybernetics** to coach your volleyball game onto the highest level possible. **Volleyball Cybernetics** will show you how to unleash the hidden power of your subconscious so that your volleyball skills and attitudes that aren't what they should be become the winning skills and attitudes you need automatically.

Now for the bad news. Unfortunately, your powerful subconscious does not always receive the best of signals because it resides within its own bottle of containment, inside the comfort zone of your self-image. Since the major supplier of feedback instruction is your self-image, expect no wish-granting magic from your subconscious unless you first free up its full potential from the bondage of a poor self-image. Understanding the importance of your self-image — that is, "the way you see yourself" as a player — means the difference between future success and failure on the court. The problem is that changing your self-image for the better isn't the easiest thing to do. It starts with changing your habits of thinking and that's a tough challenge. Remember, it took you a lifetime to shape them.

Once you improve your self-image, something else will improve that will affect your ultimate playing destiny. We're talking about your **comfort zone.** Each one of us has a personal area of thoughts and actions where we feel comfortable. Any skill or action that is new or not fully developed lies outside the comfort zone. Feel uncomfortable (pain) long enough and you tend to do only those things you can count on. Ironically, the skills and actions you need to be the player you want to be (pleasure) lie outside your current comfort zone. **Volleyball Cybernetics** will show you how to handle the **principle of pain and pleasure** to develop the ever-growing comfort zone of the winner. This means changing *I can't's* into *I can's*. It means taking risks and learning to move your body in a more confident and aggressive way even if you don't feel like it. It also means developing a new vocabulary as you speak to yourself before, during, and after competition.

Give the inner game techniques and exercises of **Volleyball Cybernetics** your best effort for three weeks; then check the results. That's all we're asking. For some of you, improvement will be immediate and dramatic. However, psychology explains that it normally takes at least 21 days for a self-image to change, so some patience may be required. Just keep in mind that our shortcut methods are time-tested. All you have to do is decide right now to give **Volleyball Cybernetics** 21 days of trust and you won't believe what happens to your game.

In competition you'll experience a feeling of confidence building within. Playing weaknesses will slowly disappear. You'll become more focused and decisive. There'll be less frustration when things go wrong. Best of all you'll be free to be the prime time player you always wanted to be.

Since 1968 **Cybernetics Training** has been helping athletes of all sports and levels live their athletic dream by showing them how to train their subconscious. Now it's your turn. Stay persistent and you can expect the following:

- **Serving:** Using our "Ultimate Serving Method," you'll consistently serve better!
- **Quickness and Aggressiveness:** You'll wonder where the new found quickness and power are coming from!
- **Power Game:** You'll play bigger and stronger at the net!
- **Defense:** You'll read the attack and dig hits you never reached before!
- **Transition Game:** You'll see the entire court and consistently find yourself in the right position!
- **Ball Handling:** You'll control the ball like never before!
- **Playing Weaknesses and Attitudes:** You'll turn glitches into glory — and with less training!
- **Clutch Performance:** You'll confidently step-up in prime time opportunities!
- **Team Work:** Team chemistry will increase!
- **Volleyball Will Be More Fun:** Without the burden of fear and frustration holding you back, you'll be free to experience the full joy of competing!

We're not finished with the promises. To get your game into the best groove possible and keep it there, you'll need to learn the **Ultimate Success Formula of Volleyball Cybernetics** called **F.A.S.T.** We promise you this proven recipe of success will activate your subconscious for full service.

If that isn't enough we'll even show you how to experience the most confident state of mind athletes are eternally seeking, **the Zone!** The key to peak performance is learning how to access and maintain this most resourceful and confident state of mind where everything you do is right, easy, and flowing. With **Cybernetics Training,** achieving this **state of flow** can be as easy as changing songs in a jukebox by simply pushing the right buttons.

Let's begin our inner journey together by looking within to learn more about your marvelous subconscious and the rest of the components of your incredible **Internal Success System.** You'll be amazed at the cooperative genie you find there. So with your dream in hand, your destiny awaits. You're about to learn how to take immediate charge of your volleyball destiny! Enjoy your inner journey.

PART ONE
In The Mind...

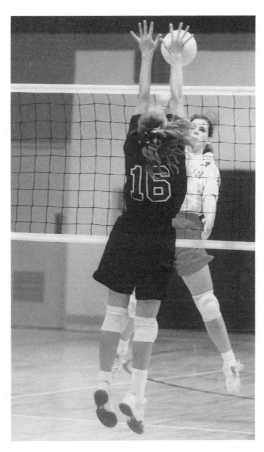

"Nothing happens unless first a dream."
Carl Sandburg

Chapter One

YOUR INTERNAL SUCCESS SYSTEM

"You are not a machine, but you have one! Discoveries in the
Science of Cybernetics all point to the conclusion that your
physical brain and nervous system make up a servo-mechanism
which operates very much like an electronic computer."
Dr. Maxwell Maltz, Author of the book *Psycho-Cybernetics*

Can you recall watching Karch Karaly quickly take an approach from the outside, go up for the attack, and at the last possible second, slow his armswing and tip the ball to an open spot on the floor for the kill? You may think you were seeing one of the world's greatest volleyball players performing with uncanny accuracy. You were actually observing a precisely programmed human computer execute its wizardry. The memory of this great athlete is stocked with thousands of past experiences of similar situations which help him evaluate present game situations. In a millisecond Karaly's subconscious mind scans both his past successes and failures and matches them to current circumstances. Simultaneously, he is perceiving the movements of others, searching for cues to an open area, locating the defense, and finally seeing the open floor. Never once does he focus his attention on his approach, become distracted by the screaming fans, or concern himself about the importance of the play. Six hundred muscles, two hundred bones, and miles of nerve fibers are activated in perfect harmony to produce an appropriate winning response. This is miraculous proof of one athlete's internal success system operating cybernetically.

Ready for this? Karch Karaly's Internal Success System operates exactly the same as the one you have. We mean exactly.

3

THE WORLD'S GREATEST COMPUTER SYSTEM

The road **Volleyball Cybernetics** takes you on leads straight to the control center for all performance, your mind. No Freudian approach here, your brain and nervous system are examined cybernetically as the world's greatest computer system.

The learning process will include:
1. Understanding the capabilities and laws of your biological computer
2. Discovering the key operational rules of your mental computer's power mechanism — the subconscious
3. Learning all about the focusing device inside your mental computer — the **Reticular Activating System**

The comparison of the human brain and the electronic computer has been scientifically established. Let's look at how your brain receives, processes, and records the signals it uses to produce your volleyball game. Everything you do or have ever done on the court, every thought, every sight, sound, and feeling are stored inside your mental computer. Your past playing experiences are indelibly recorded in the memory bank of your inner computer. Their job is to become vital feedback signals (mental recordings) to be used by your subconscious to create future action on the court.

PERSONAL REPRESENTATIONS

These mental recordings are not always accurate. They are your personal representations, interpretations, and impressions of your playing experiences. They are not always reality. If you have the habit of editing your impressions with a negative spin or focus, chances are you're guilty of storing the wrong kind of software inside your head, and you can expect a sentence punishable by a lifetime of underachievement. Insert the wrong kind of software into any top of the line IBM computer and you won't get the right time of day. The cybernetic law states, **Input determines output.** This law also applies to your game. It's true that you become what you think. That's why success breeds success and failure breeds frustration. **Garbage in...garbage out!** says the computer programmer, and the smart coach agrees.

Your best chance for tapping your full potential is to stack as many positive internal representations as you can into your mental computer. Unless you start thinking, feeling, talking, and especially interpreting in a positive way, you can be certain your play will remain inconsistent. **Before you run out of games to play, you ought to take a hard look at what you're putting into cold storage inside your inner computer. Whatever it is, your destiny is being shaped by it.**

With the help of the methods of **Volleyball Cybernetics,** you'll store thousands of success signals in the quickest time frame possible. With the short-cut methods of mental visualization, power talk, positive affirmations, modeling, and "acting as if," you'll have more than enough mental recordings to earn a ticket into the winner's circle.

THERE'S NOTHING WRONG WITH YOUR COMPUTER

Even if you think you're the number one underachiever on your team, there's absolutely nothing wrong with the operational ability of your internal computer. The key will be to see, imagine, feel, talk, and remember in a positive way so that your **Internal Success System** will be able to operate at full power. Just take a look at its potential and you can start counting your blessings.

- Your human brain contains more storage cells than the largest man-made computer. At the latest estimation, you have over 100 billion storage cells ready to store an infinite amount of winning instructions.
- Your brain needs only two basic ingredients to operate, sugar and oxygen. The last time we looked, both were highly available and inexpensive.
- Brain repairs are rarely needed. Not so for its mechanical counterpart. Factor in a thousand watts of expensive electrical energy and costly repairs for the man-made machine.
- Science cannot build a facsimile of your human computer (they're trying but can't). When they do (which they won't), the cost would be in the billions!
- In 3-1/2 pounds and 6 inches of corrugated organ, your human brain contains over 7,000 miles of wiring, is capable of accepting at least 16 new facts for every second of your life, and has the ability of sending instructions to over 200 muscles more rapidly than any electronic computer could ever process a response.

Are you impressed? You should be. The undeniable fact is that you own the greatest, most miraculous, incomparable gift of pure potentiality sitting between your ears. **And the best part is it's user friendly!**

DON'T KNOCK YOURSELF: JUST REPROGRAM!

Would you throw away an expensive IBM computer if you weren't getting correct responses? Certainly not. Would you insult it or call it all kinds of names if it failed you? You could, but it would be a waste of time. The smart thing would be to examine its software and replace it with better information.

That's exactly what you are about to do to improve your game. By learning our inner game strategies for programming better software into your mental computer, the sky just may be the limit!

SAY HELLO TO YOUR FRIENDLY GENIE

Time to meet your success mechanism. Yes, there is a genie within your computer with enough muscle power to perform all kinds of successful events for you on the court. Look at all of the good stuff it's capable of doing:

1. Your subconscious is the mental engineer that handles all of your autonomic, life-saving bodily functions, such as controlling blood pressure, pulse rate, breathing rhythm, swallowing, sneezing, digestion and muscle reflex. These are just a few of the services it renders

on a 24-hour basis; it never sleeps. The tireless subconscious is always on call.

2. Your subconscious is responsible for remembering and producing all of your learned habits, from walking to all of your favorite and not so favorite volleyball skills.

3. Your subconscious has a creative side with a capacity to produce a full range of feelings and expectations. Its inventive powers can construct or destroy your volleyball dream in a heartbeat.

For example, let's say you're back to serve with your team down 12-14 in the final game of the match. The line judge rolls you the ball. Because you missed your last serve earlier in the game, you're not in the most confident state of mind. Noticing a tightening feeling of anxiety building within your body, you try to push the past out of your mind by taking a deep breath and slowly exhaling. The official whistles for the serve. You focus hard on the ball in your hands for a second or two longer than usual. The harder you concentrate, the more time you have to remember that serving in pressure situations is not one of your strengths. Not only do your parents sitting in the stands know your tendency to fold under pressure (they're praying), your coach knows (she's sweating up a storm), the opposition knows (they're preparing to celebrate), but worst of all, your subconscious also knows it and has already gone to work, producing a feeling of anxiety.

Somehow you make the first serve and your team wins the rally to make it 13-14. However, the second serve, which never felt right, goes into the net. The culprit is your subconscious. Knowing that you never put together a string of winning serves in pressure situations, you compensate by overtrying which is not the best order to convey to your obedient servant. Reading your concern, the subconscious, faithful to a fault, overtries by sending out more signals than are necessary. The wrong muscles of your arms respond by tightening up. As muscle fights muscle, the outcome is a low toss and a flat, line drive served directly into the net. **Thanks to the creative powers of your subconscious, you programmed yourself to successfully miss the serve!**

How Your Subconscious Turns Out Habits

Identical to any cybernetic machine, your cybernetic device demands two basic ingredients:

1. Clear-cut goals
2. Information signals

As creative and powerful as it is, your faithful servant is impersonal. The subconscious does not care what you tell it to do; its job is to just get it done. Whether you give it goals of success, "This is what I want to do," or goals of fear "This is what I want to avoid," it operates with detached indifference. Your first step will be to present your **subconscious** with only positive goals.

Then there is the problem of asking your subconscious to perform spectacularly without giving it spectacular input signals. **Improve input and output improves** is our cybernetic formula. The cybernetic process involves upgrading the quality of input you store in the memory bank of your biological computer. Rethink any feelings you have of being inferior, undeserving, and unworthy of success. Learn, practice, and experience new habits of thinking, imagining, remembering, and acting in order to improve your self-image. Are you ready to do the following?

1. **Rethink all limiting beliefs into unlimiting beliefs.**
2. **Learn to move your body in a more confident manner by modeling the best and then learning how to "act as if."**
3. **Introduce a steady stream of "Yes, I Can" self-talk statements and develop the habit of asking yourself empowering questions.**

As your beliefs, body movements, and self-talk change for the better, it will be your self-image and its accompanying comfort zone that enjoy the benefits. Don't be surprised to find a very liberated, appreciative, and cooperative genie suddenly appear in your life. You may find yourself taking more risks on the court and finishing plays like never before.

How The Subconscious Turns Out Your Playing Habits

Picture in your mind a wishing well. You remember, like the one in "Jack and Jill." Now imagine your conscious mind as the *bucket* hanging on the rope above the deep, vast *well* that represents your subconscious mind. As you are learning a new skill, most of the learning is happening in the *bucket* or the conscious mind. Once you become more competent and confident with that skill, it overflows the bucket and goes down into the *well* or the subconscious mind. Let's think of an example:

Think about when you learned to ride a two-wheeled bike. At first, you were totally in the bucket. *Dad or Mom were running with you holding on to the back of the seat as you were pleading, "Don't let go!" After a number of attempts, you were cruising along, and discovered that they had let go and were a half block behind you. While you were cruising, you were in the* well *just letting it happen. As soon as you realized that you were on your own, you instantly switched back to the* bucket *and lacking the confidence, you crashed!*

Now that you have mastered the skill of riding a bike, you do it entirely from the well. *You don't have to think about it; you just do it!*

In your volleyball game, the same principles are at work. Let's look at the skill of serving. When you first learn how to serve, you are totally in the *bucket*. You are conscious of everything you do — how to stand, how to toss and hit the ball, how far away the net is, how embarrassed you are going to be when the ball goes flying anywhere but where it's supposed to. Every time you serve the ball successfully, more of that success overflows from the *bucket* into the *well*. As you become a good server, a winning habit is produced and the subconscious (or the *well*) takes over to duplicate that skill whenever you let it. So, let's look at the master secret of **Volleyball Cybernetics** to learn how to fill up your *bucket* with successes and allow it to overflow into your *well* of confidence and competence.

The Master Secret Of Volleyball Cybernetics

Do you realize that **the subconscious cannot tell the difference between a real and a vividly imagined experience!** That's great news since you're in charge of your own imagination. Think about the endless options that this fantastic insight provides for programming your subconscious. The key to improving your game will be to control your imagination, rather than allowing your imagination to control you.

Just as computer scientists discovered that computers accept wrong information, brain scientists learned that the nervous system cannot always tell the difference between an imagined or real experience. Again, man and machine share a common law of behavior. There is nothing supernatural about watching a hypnotized 200 pound weightlifter suddenly become incapable of lifting a pencil off a table. What you're witnessing is the normal operating process of the human brain and nervous system accepting an imagined belief, and responding to it as if it were an absolute truth.

MENTAL PRACTICE MAKES PERFECT

Behavioral psychologists have long been aware of the influence of imagined experiences. A classic study of the effects was reported in *Research Quarterly* over 40 years ago. The subject was mental practice in free throw shooting. Using three groups of non-basketball players, one group practiced foul shooting every day for 20 days and was scored on the first and last day. A second group did not practice at all and was scored on the first and last day. The third group also was scored on the first and last day, but spent the 18 days in between imagining themselves shooting one successful shot after another for 20 minutes a day.

What happened was pure cybernetics. As expected, the group that didn't practice didn't improve. Amazingly, the group that trained mentally improved by 23% — almost the same improvement that was achieved by the group that physically practiced shooting free throws (24%). Can you imagine the results when you combine the mental practice with the physical?

Want more proof about the effects of mental practice? Clinical psychologists have recorded the impulse responses of athletes who were mentally summoning up the moment by moment imagery of their favorite skiing event. The researchers attached an electromylograph to the muscles of these athletes while they were visualizing themselves performing. Electrical signals were being received and recorded by their muscles as if the athletes were actually experiencing the event. The conclusion was that muscle memory can be experienced as a result of an imagined event.

READY FOR A FIRST PERSON EXPERIENCE?

Want to experience the influence of mental practice right now? Try this: stand up and fully extend your right arm forward, pointing your index finger straight ahead. Keep your left hand at your side. Make sure your right arm and wrist are perfectly straight and your feet are solidly planted on the floor shoulder width apart. In a clockwise direction, see how far you can twist and turn around the upper part of your body without moving your feet. Swing the extended arm around with the pointer finger leading the way. Notice exactly how far you're capable of turning. Remember the exact location on the wall behind you where you were able to point.

Now using the power of imagination, see how much further you can twist. Rest both arms at your side and close your eyes. Imagine your right arm is extended in front of you with the index finger pointed. Can you imagine feeling its weight? Now only in your mind, visualize that you are twisting your upper body as you bring your arm around clockwise. This time **feel** that you are capable of comfortably turning your body well beyond the point that you achieved earlier on the real try. Mentally rehearse the successful twist several times more, each time twisting further around.

Time to retest. Now do it again physically. Extend your right arm, pointing your index finger forward, and see how much further you can swing the arm around.

Surprised at the outcome? You shouldn't be. Shakespeare said, **"Imagination rules your world."** Our question to you is, **"Are you ready to rule your imagination?"**

HOW TO GET YOUR SUBCONSCIOUS TO WORK FOR YOU

1. Never worry about or be afraid of making mistakes. This leads to hesitation and a lack of aggressiveness. Skill learning is achieved by trial and error, so simply do your best to improve. Forget errors, remember successes.

2. See your goals as accomplished facts. Remember your subconscious does not know the difference between a real and imagined event. **Act as if** success has already been achieved, and you'll soon be enjoying the results.

3. Trust your subconscious to work. Overtrying only leads to underachieving. Easy does it. **Let it work,** rather than **make it work.** More about this later.

4. Focus on positive thoughts and expectations of success. Never say or think, "I can't do this." ("I can't" really means "I won't.") Instead, tell yourself, **"I CAN!"** More often than not, we get what we expect.

5. Visualization exercises are most effective when your mind and body are totally relaxed and ready for sleep.

6. Your subconscious keeps working even after you have fallen asleep. Present it with a problem while awaiting sleep and by morning you'll have a solution. (See the **Sleep On It** technique on page 152).

YOUR FOCUSING DEVICE: THE RETICULAR ACTIVATING SYSTEM

Without sharpening your focusing skills, you can forget about your volleyball dream or any other dream of success. The master skill is concentration; that's your ability to become fully aware of what is important and what isn't in the heat of action. The winner stays in the **here and now;** the loser lives in the past or future, or becomes easily distracted by the nonessential. Nothing wrong with looking into the past for learning lessons or thinking ahead to plan your action, but in competition, centering your energy in the present is a must.

This brings us to another primary fixture of your **Inner Success System** — your **Reticular Activating System (RAS).** Master this mechanism of success and you master life! Study the winners and you'll find people who know how to correctly use the focusing powers of their **RAS** and stay in the **here and now.**

To prove this point try picturing a plank of wood 18 inches wide and 50 feet in length. Think about placing this plank on the floor and walking its length. No big deal. You'd do it in a second if asked. Would you take $50 as a reward if offered? Certainly. Now what if we offered you $50 to walk this same foot and a half wide plank, but this time the plank was placed between two high rise buildings, say 40 stories high. Would you do it? We think not! We'll even increase the prize to $1000. Still not ready to take the risk?

Why not? Because you're imagining the worst possible outcome, aren't you? Death, perhaps! Instead of centering your attention confidently on the accommodating width of plank as you did earlier, you'd probably become aware of all kinds of extraneous factors: the slightest movement of the wind, the noise of the traffic below, the queasy feeling in the pit of your stomach, and the unsureness of your legs. Rather than think success as you did with the plank on the floor, your mind might drift off to the sound of a body hitting pavement. An imagined sound of "Splat!" does not provide the best instructions for your subconscious to hear.

In competition, are you easily distracted by the movements of opposing players? Does the crowd, the score, fatigue, or your last poor hitting attempt rattle you? Without disciplining the filtering service of your RAS, your subconscious will continue to be bombarded with a litany of useless and distracting signals.

Is prime time performance your dream? Then it's time to develop your **focusing facilitator.** The game of volleyball offers a kaleidoscopic series of continually changing action. Countless sights, sounds, feelings, and actions are simultaneously occurring during every second of play. The infinite power of your subconscious is wasted unless your eyes, ears, mind, and body are centered on the task at hand. Your conscious mind can focus on a limited number of elements at any one moment in time, so what you focus on must be relative to the success of your action. Focus on what is irrelevant and your performance is in trouble. With an out-of-control **RAS,** your play will remain inconsistent. Here are some **"Yes, I Can!" Camp** experiences that illustrate how athletes elevated their game by taking control of their **RAS** to screen in the essential and screen out the unnecessary.

• There was the player who had great difficulty reading an attack angle and setting a correct block. When she learned how to successfully switch focus from the flight of the set to the path of the hitter's approach, she became capable of consistently setting and executing winning blocks. This was something she was unable to do, until she sharpened her focusing skill.

• Another athlete with the habit of shanking her digs found success by reading the hitter's approach angle first, and then moving her body into the line of attack.

• When a poor server developed her ability to focus on a new mind set of **letting it happen** rather than **making it happen,** she suddenly found that the flight of her serve traveled in a stronger, more accurate trajectory.

• One of the most amazing camp stories of success was the 16 year old girl who mastered the screening powers of her **RAS** to achieve her highest priority goal, to eliminate a nine month long tension headache. Instead of focusing on what was right with her game and the rest of the world, our **perfectionist** camper had the habit of centering her attention only on what went wrong. Her **RAS** cooperated by filtering out the good and keying in on her miscues and the associated pain that went with it. She punished herself by piling so much toxic garbage into her mental computer, that her head began to pound with such pain that life had become unbearable. Finally at camp, she learned to pay attention to the positive and let go of the negative. Forced into a mind set of **looking for good,** her headache disappeared as mysteriously as it had come.

There have been countless athletes at camp who have improved their game soon after sharpening their ability to focus on what they wanted and not on what they wanted to avoid. With the concentration and relaxation exercises of **Volleyball Cybernetics,** your **RAS** soon will be free to unleash its full power.

Now that you've been told about the reliability and creative powers of your **Internal Success System's** physical parts, let's examine its equally powerful psychological components. Up next, the **self-image** and its home, the **comfort zone**. Together they carry a powerful punch capable of either knocking out your volleyball dream or giving you the inner strength needed to become the best player you can be.

Chapter Two

THE PSYCHOLOGICAL COMPONENTS OF YOUR INTERNAL SUCCESS SYSTEM

"Construct a better self image and you have a golden key
for living a better life."
Dr. Maxwell Maltz

THE SELF IMAGE

The mental picture you have of yourself, the kind of performer you consider yourself to be, is your self-image. Believe us when we tell you that nothing is more crucial to your volleyball performance than **"the way you think about yourself."**

Close your eyes and think about a weak offensive skill that frustrates you almost every time you're forced to use it in competition. Imagine that you're playing in a game with the score tied at 14. The ball finds you and you're forced to execute this weak offensive skill, for example, an attack down the line. What did you picture in your mind? Did you see yourself finishing the play, or did you see yourself messing it up? If you're honest, the expectation wasn't positive, was it?

Sitting in the director's chair of this unhappy ending is none other than your self-image. Continue to define your game with negative images and self-talk, and your performance will continue to be limited and inconsistent. The first step on your journey of success starts with being aware of the power of your self-image as the key supplier of software instructions to your subconscious.

A System Of Beliefs

Like we said, your self-image may not be a true statement of your potential and talent because it's based on impressions of your past experiences rather than fact. With a negative focus your impressions can easily become **a darkened deception of reality rather than a description of the way things are.**

Your past experiences started on the first day you began to play volleyball. Naturally they included both successes and failures. When the mistakes outnumbered the completions, you began to form a belief that your mistakes were standard behavior. Perhaps your parents, coaches, or teammates displayed a negative reaction when you played poorly. Any wrong glance, facial expression, or a verbal put-down further contributed to a growing feeling that you were not the most natural athlete around. To make matters worse, you foolishly compared yourself to an older brother, sister or the team's star.

The Forces That Shape Your Self-Image

"Everything you do is either out of a need to avoid pain or a desire to gain pleasure," writes Anthony Robbins, the noted self-help guru and author of the book **Awaken The Giant Within.** So often we hear stories about athletes who have talent but are unable to take action when the game is on the line. They would like to, but for some reason can't get themselves to "just do it!" They've never learned to control the two most powerful forces that shape their self-image. Please accept this as a given: **unless you understand and use the forces of pain and pleasure to your advantage, you'll never become the player you want to be. The forces of pain and pleasure will use you!**

Think we're exaggerating the point? Answer these questions. Why don't you train harder and longer, stop your procrastination, or take more risks on the court? What's holding you back from doing the aggressive things you should be doing? The answer: there's less pain in taking a passive approach than in taking action. Of course you realize that taking action will be beneficial and in the long run bring you pleasure, but you fail to **do the thing that's hard to do,** because at that moment you're thinking **pain avoidance.** So you do what has become easy and natural. You do nothing! With the techniques of **Volleyball Cybernetics,** we'll show you how to make **pain and pleasure** a best friend instead of your worst enemy.

Shaping A Negative Self-Image For Spiking

Do you remember when you first learned how to spike? You were enthusiastic and hopeful. You hit a lot of balls in bounds and missed a lot, too. You noticed that each successful spike created a good feeling inside. You also noticed that when you tried to spike the ball really hard, you'd hit more balls out of bounds or in the net than you put in play. A feeling of disappointment after each miss discouraged you from making a commitment to working on spiking the ball hard. It was easier and

13

more rewarding to ease up on your swing, and keep the ball in play than to try to spike the ball hard, fail, and feel bad. That's the **pain and pleasure principle** controlling your response.

You may have contributed further to an evolving negative self-image by overreacting to the responses of teammates. When opportunities arose in key game situations in order to avoid these painful responses of others, you made it a habit not to aggressively call for the set. Whenever you did jump and swing hard with an unproductive outcome, you concluded that your skills were limited. The few times that you did spike the ball hard for a kill, you credited your success to pure luck. All proof that a limited self-image has been created. Until you can improve the way you **see yourself** spiking, and learn how to handle the **pain and pleasure principle,** your play will continue to be tentative.

WHY THE POWER OF POSITIVE THINKING WON'T WORK ALONE

Self-image psychology explains why using the power of positive thinking alone won't work with poor performing athletes. A three-pronged attack is required. When positive thinking is used without positive body language and self-talk, the negative self-image is still in charge. To improve the self-image, positive thinking must be aligned with appropriate body language and self-talk. Without all three working in harmony, all the pep talks, positive thinking, expert coaching or hoping won't help.

HOW TO INSTANTLY OVERCOME A NEGATIVE SELF-IMAGE

The family car that the two young brothers were working on was parked in the driveway. With its front wheels removed, the Chevy Impala was precariously supported by three cinder blocks under its front axle. The younger brother was working underneath the front end of the car changing the oil when the car suddenly shifted and slid off the supporting blocks. Suddenly 3,500 pounds of steel came crashing down on the younger brother beginning to crush the life from his body. The older brother, Tom, hearing the cry for help instantly realized what he had to do. Quickly Tom managed to somehow lift up the front bumper just long enough to enable his brother to safely roll out from beneath the car. This amazing event happened in the fall of 1968 right before the first championship season of Stan Kellner's high school basketball team. To this day Stan feels that this single miraculous incident, more than any other, was responsible for his team's run of championship seasons and subsequent development of **Cybernetics Training.** In fact, the book you have in your hands would not have been written had Tom not found that extraordinary surge of hidden power.

Let Stan tell you why:

"Tom was a student in my physical education class who flat out could not complete ten consecutive push ups. He didn't have enough strength to climb the gym rope more than 10 feet or hand travel across the parallel bars without collapsing. No exaggeration, Tom was one of the meekest, weakest 135 pounders I ever had in my class. Then all of a sudden, he became a hero saving his brother by lifting the front end of a 3,500 pound car. An instant transformation from hopeless to hero! I couldn't believe it. When Tom came to school the day after the miraculous event, he was so bent out of shape with a strained back that he looked like Quasimoto. When I asked him how he managed to accomplish the feat, he told me when he saw his brother being crushed by the weight of the car, the power to lift the car was just there. He said he had no trouble lifting the front end of the car.

Of course, Tom's instant strength can be explained as an example of the **fight or flight syndrome.** Science explains that whenever we perceive a threat, our body automatically responds to the danger by preparing itself for the emergency. When Tom heard his brother's plea for help, his body's endocrine system immediately excreted a chemical called adrenaline which excited his large muscles to perform beyond their normal capacity. Plus Tom's circulatory system contributed by directing more blood to his arms and legs further readying him for a super performance.

As impressed as I was with Tom's success story, the question I had was, "If Tom had this range of power with this enormous reserve, why couldn't he tap his automatic fight or flight system to work for him in PE class, or anywhere else, when some personal power was needed?" Being a coach, with an annually underachieving team, I couldn't help but wonder why my players, much like Tom, couldn't find their overdrive gear to achieve in the emergencies of a game. I also had to find an answer to another question racing through my mind. **Is there a way we can tell our body what we want our body to do, when we want our body to do it, or does our body always tell us what it wants?** For my players, it seemed that it was their bodies that were doing the talking. I had to know, was there a language or a process that could tell my players how to communicate with their bodies so that they could perform like winners? If Tom could instantly display the power to tell his body what he needed from it, what about my free throw shooter who had trouble converting when the game was on the line, or my rebounder who couldn't hold on to the ball in traffic, or my mild-mannered center who was unwilling to take a charge or dive for a loose ball? What about their sad stories? If Tom could step up as a hero, why couldn't they? If there was a way, I had to know.

My search started by reading books on kinesiology, physiology, even way out books on Eastern philosophies. But it wasn't until I read the self-help books and found Maxwell Maltz's classic book **Psycho-Cybernetics** that I found what I wanted. Little did I know at the time that this simple text of self-discovery would literally change my life and the lives of my players. Not only did I learn what had held Tom back from achieving in physical education class, I realized what was holding me back from becoming a winning coach. I became excited about the possibilities it offered for getting my players to play with more aggressiveness, confidence, and success. Dr. Maltz had combined the Science of Cybernetics with Self-image Psychology to create a handbook of success that could guide people to achieve anything they really wanted for themselves. I wondered if it would work for my players?

After reading a few chapters on the potential of the subconscious and the influence of the self-image, I understood that it was Tom's poor self-image that had kept him from achieving in gym class. Without a reason big enough to drive Tom and his cybernetic-performing subconscious to overcome his inadequate self-image, he had no other choice but to underachieve. When faced with the strong possibility of his brother's death and the massive pain he would experience unless he took action, Tom's subconscious transcended his 'I can't' self-image and was elevated to full power."

Are you ready to overcome your habits of negative thinking and replace them with empowering patterns that can build your self-image? Do you have a reason big enough to free up your powerful subconscious to achieve the skills and attitudes you want? We hope so, because you'll need one if you expect to improve another psychological essential of your internal success system. There is something you are trained to honor more than success itself. We're talking about your **comfort zone.**

THE COMFORT ZONE

Your comfort zone doesn't exist physically, but because of the **"pain and pleasure principle"** it's there determining the exact degree of your on-the-court success. Because it's the permanent home of your self-image, one of the best ways to improve the way you think about yourself is to expand your comfort zone. Improve one and the other improves. With an "I can" self-image, you have a growing comfort zone. With an expanding comfort zone you have an improving self-image. Do something everyday in practice or a match that is hard to do and both the self-image and comfort zone grow. So will your game.

Just imagine your comfort zone as a circle of fear. Losers consider it a wall of protection. Within this wall are your current volleyball skills and attitudes which bring you the most success. Because you played them so many times with predictable results, you feel comfortable performing these playing habits in competition. The problem with a narrow comfort zone is that the skills and attitudes that will allow you to live your volleyball dream lie outside its walls.

Overachievers operate out of an unlimited comfort zone. They're unafraid to work on new types of offensive shots, to go for that "impossible" dig, or a more aggressive serve. Mistakes are never permanent. Pain is no big deal either. What is vital is the payoff down the road, not the temporary discomfort of hard work, or the physical pain. You'll always find these athletes challenging themselves to do difficult things on the court, like hitting down the line or serving tough to the corner for a crucial point in the match. Instead of feeling threatened by the fear of embarrassment, the course of uncertainty inspires them. Sure they feel the fear as we all do, but they just do it anyway. They play through the fear, and the power to take action is always there.

Most athletes play it safe and stay within the perimeter of their comfort zone. Their habit is to use the same serve and hit to the same spots. They always hit or tip with the same strong hand and find themselves underhand passing a free ball when they should have taken the risk with a more accurate overhand pass. **A great definition of insanity is doing the same things over and over again and expecting better results.** Continue to play within the wall of your comfort zone and the past will equal the future. No matter what you try to imagine or say to yourself, progress will be impossible. Risks and pain must be experienced. The chains of your comfort zone have to be broken. **"No pain, no gain"** is absolutely correct. Every time you challenge yourself, every time you feel that feeling of uncertainty in the pit of your stomach, your comfort zone is expanding. It's time to stop hiding behind old habits like anxiety, frustration, fatigue, injuries, and fear. They all have one thing in common. They're a great waste of energy. Make them vanish by living by this new code of behavior: **"to have what you have not...you must do what you have not done!"**

How To Expand Your Comfort Zone

Here are nine steps you can take for comfort zone expansion:

1. Value success over entertainment.
2. Set goals that are challenging.
3. Develop a feeling of certainty that success is inevitable.
4. Make it a habit **to do the thing that is hard to do.**
5. When you feel the fear, do it anyway.
6. Learn how to turn frustration into fascination.
7. Eliminate the word *try* from your playing vocabulary.
8. Do it now! Strike procrastination from life's game plan.
9. Use the **pain and pleasure** principle to work for you.

Value success over entertainment: Think ahead about the pleasure of success first. Make entertainment a distant second. Whenever you have a choice between entertainment (such as hanging out with your friends or watching TV) or success (such as achieving a daily quota of 100 push-ups, 100 sit-ups, making 50 serves or setting the ball to yourself 500 times), decide to take the positive action of hard work.

Set goals that are challenging: Be on the hunt for training or performance goals that challenge you, that allow you to grow; then go for it! Consider every goal as a once in a lifetime, extraordinary opportunity. Don't live your life as if it's going to last forever. Forget the cliché, "Today is the first day of the rest of my life." Rather, live each day as if it were your last. Play with passion. Train with a sense of intense urgency, with no pacing allowed! Give an all out effort every second you train or compete. And while you are at it, put this sign, "I'm out achieving...won't be back!" in front of your television set at home.

Develop a feeling of certainty that success is inevitable: What would you do on the court if you couldn't fail? Achievers live with the feeling that success is waiting for them down the road and failure is not in the realm of possibility. They have that strong and clear inner picture of what they want to accomplish. To them setbacks are not only temporary but wonderful opportunities for growth. They never seem to lose their energy and enthusiasm to forge ahead no matter what price they must pay. They know how to use their imagination as an ally because they have the ability to see what they want, not what they want to avoid.

Make it a habit to do the thing that is hard to do: Whenever you have an opportunity to choose between doing something that is easy or difficult in training or a match, make the tough choice and do the hard thing. Each time you do, you are expanding your comfort zone. Expect the power to be there and it will!

17

Feel the fear and do it anyway: Anytime you experience fear, fatigue, boredom, embarrassment or a feeling of unworthiness realize their benefits. You are at the edge of your comfort zone. That's great! Now that you know where you are, feel the pain and do it anyway. These feelings of discomfort are the proof that you're taking a risk and are about to escape your comfort zone. Risks must be taken if you are to grow as a person and as an athlete. By the way, let's rename that feeling of fear you experience before games. Call it by its real name, **excitement.** It's nature's way of preparing you for success!

Turn frustration into fascination: When you feel frustrated as a result of a setback or disappointment, turn the negative into a positive by asking yourself this empowering question: "What's good about it?" or this one: "What have I learned here, so this outcome does not recur?" Asking smart questions helps you stay on track.

Eliminate the word "try" from your playing vocabulary: Stay away from the word try. **Try** is a three-letter word for comfort zone effort. **"I'll try"** qualifies you for an early **quit.**

Do it now! Strike procrastination from life's game plan: Procrastination is another disempowering technique for keeping your game in a holding pattern. If you have a habit of putting things off until tomorrow, you ought to understand what **tomorrow** really is: It's a road called **Someday** that leads to a town called **Nowhere!** Our advice is, "If you must procrastinate, procrastinate tomorrow"! One thing for sure, if you do travel this often-traveled road you'll never be alone. There'll be a crowd of underachievers traveling along with you.

Use the Pain and Pleasure Principle to work for you: Motivate yourself by utilizing the **Pain and Pleasure Principle** to your advantage. This principle teaches us that basic motivation comes from one of two sources — either the need to avoid pain or the desire to gain pleasure. Of the two, the need to avoid pain is a much greater motivator for most people. Now let's see how this knowledge can work to your benefit.

Since your brain naturally wants to avoid physical pain, such as muscle soreness, you need to reframe or redefine the meaning of that soreness. Let's define soreness as simply the strengthening and expanding of our muscles. Then, you can focus on the benefits of those stronger muscles — making you faster, making you healthier, reducing your chances of injuries, etc. That same *pain* that you now call muscle expansion may be your admission to the winner's circle. Make it your habit to project ahead to the payoff that awaits your unrelenting commitment to hard work and risk taking. Make sure that the picture of *pleasure* you create in your mind is vastly more motivating and lasting than the temporary discomfort of *pain*. Remember the only meaning that something (such as pain) has, is the meaning that **you give it!**

So, whenever you're faced with a tough decision on or off the court and you have a choice to either take the tough road or the easy one, review this list of winning suggestions for comfort zone expansion. What strategy do you think motivated Karch Karaly into greatness? Talent alone? Was it the lure of fame and fortune? Don't bet on it. Check the list again and you will have Karaly's strategy for achievement.

THE COMFORT ZONE JUNKIE WITHIN

There is a **Comfort Zone Junkie** that lurks within all of us. The addiction is subtle. You can never tell when you've become one until it's too late and your career is over. Then you realize there is nothing to look back on with pride.

How do you know if you're a **Comfort Zone Junkie?** There are two tell-tale signs. First, you're pretty much satisfied with your game. Second, a fear of making a mistake follows you where ever you go on the court. You'll do most anything to avoid making a playing mistake including hiding from the ball when the game is on the line.

Watch out for these symptoms. You are an addict when you...

C   **Consider** weaknesses as permanent
O   **Overtry** in competition...but undertry in practice
M   **Make** security your #1 priority
F   **Frustrate** quickly
O   **Overconcern** yourself about results
R   **Remember** mistakes
T   **Try** with comfort zone effort

Z   **Zero** in on what's wrong
O   **Overwhelm** yourself with too much thinking
N   **Negate** the positive
E   **Excuse** things quickly

Breaking any addiction starts with the awareness that you are an addict. Here are our addiction breaking steps that you can take:

C   **Consider** playing weaknesses as opportunities to grow
O   **Overwork** in practice
M   **Make** success your #1 priority
F   **Free up** from frustration by refusing to be disappointed by mistakes
O   **Overtake** your concern with positive thinking
R   **Remember** to focus on what you do right
T   **Take action until you** get what you want

Z   **Zero** in on your goal
O   **Overlook** what overwhelms you
N   **Nurture** your self-image with power thoughts, questions, and deeds
E   **Excite** yourself with challenges that allow you to grow

Are you willing to live these suggestions as Alcoholics Anonymous recommends, **one day at a time?** Well, then do it, and discover a hidden reserve of talent that you've always had. **Your Comfort Zone Junkie days are over.**

JUST DO IT!

Several years ago, while coaching a 16 and under team for the Victors Volleyball Club, Coach Mike Gibson wanted to expand the comfort zones of his players. In doing so, he also helped them conquer the most common fear among young female volleyball players – the fear of being embarrassed.

At their next practice, he announced that they were going to learn a skill that was new to the entire team – jump serving. Mike explained to the girls that it was a weapon they would all need to have during the season to become successful as a team. Through trial and error the team learned to jump serve, eventually using their new found skill in a scrimmage at the end of practice.

After winning the first game of their opening match in the next tournament, Coach Mike announced that in game two everyone on the team was going to jump serve — every serve. The looks of disbelief were everywhere. Next came the excuses — all the reasons that they couldn't possibly complete that request. Mike informed them that it was not a request, but rather a requirement for competing in the game and that the first six players who were up to the task should get on the floor. Sheepishly, six comfort zone expanders took the challenge and entered the game. The rest of the bench was later subbed in so everyone could share in the *enjoyment*.

As the game progressed, the girls served up many varieties of the jump serve — over the net and in bounds, over the net but out of bounds, into the net, under the net, one that almost knocked the ref off the stand, and the worst of all — a swing and a miss. The Victors managed to lead through most of the game in spite of their erratic serving. When the other team reeled off several points to tie the game at 12-12, Mike called a time out. The team was expecting him to call off the jump serving rule for the rest of the game and go for the win, but that wasn't "Gib's" intent. Instead, he told them to focus on serving successfully and keep jump serving.

The Victors ended up winning the game 16-14 – on a jump serve ace! By the end of the season most of the team was jump serving regularly in each match. The players had expanded their comfort zones and diminished their fears of being embarrassed to a point of being able to play free and relaxed. The results were that the team finished in the top four at the state finals, one of the best seasons in the history of the club.

NO PAIN... NO GAIN

Pain has its benefits in more ways than one. You can never tell when it just might win you a big game. From 1989 to 1993, the Penn State Men's team was to college volleyball what the Buffalo Bills were to the NFL. During that span the Nittany Lions and their coach, Tom Peterson, made it to the NCAA Final Four four times only to lose in the semi-finals to a West Coast team. If that wasn't bad enough, they were beaten in three straight games each year!

Shortly after their loss to Cal State at Northridge in the 1993 Semis, Coach Peterson was quoted in *Volleyball Monthly*, "Our problems have to do with our level of confidence. We have to play like we played all year in our conference and not play scared. If we were in the Mountain Pacific (Sports Federation) there would be no surprises. We would be comfortable. Somehow we've got to get that across to our players."

When the smoke cleared in the 1994 season and the Final Four was again ready to go, there was Penn State once again playing in the "Big Dance." For the fifth time in six years the Nittany Lions had made it. But this time they had found the necessary extra edge to make it to the Finals and from an unlikely source...the **Pain and Pleasure Principle.** The carrot (pleasure), of course, was the joy of winning a National Championship. The stick (pain) in this case was to have an even more powerful influence. Beyond their talent and an enduring belief in themselves, they had an incredible sense of purpose, a total sense of commitment to their mission to do whatever was necessary to finish the tournament season without a loss. Their outside hitter, Ed Josefski, expressed it best when he was quoted in *Volleyball Monthly* early in the season predicting Penn State would win the National Championship. He said, "We are sick of finishing third and fourth. My parents told me if we get a third or fourth place trophy not to bring it home."

The Lions defeated Ball State in the semi-finals to reach the championship match for the first time. However, things did not go well for them at the beginning of the final match. They lost two of the first three games against the high flying UCLA Bruins and were trailing in game four by a score of 4-11; but they didn't panic. What happened next was an incredible comeback that led to what many volleyball fans have called one of the biggest upsets in sports history. Penn State somehow regrouped and rallied to win the National Championship by a final score of 9-15, 15-13, 4-15, 15-12, 15-12! Was it their talent and confidence alone that got them into the winner's circle? Maybe, but when their backs were to the wall and they were about to be put away, they had another advantage going for them. The thought of coming home without a championship trophy was too much to tolerate. They exploded out of their comfort zone and cut loose to play the best volleyball of their lives.

The next time you experience the pain of a tough loss remember that lousy feeling for future reference. And say, "This has got to stop." Value the pain of the loss by telling yourself... "No pain...no gain." Consider pain a great friend for comfort zone expansion, that is if you've got "guts to get out of the ruts." If Penn State can win a National Championship by thinking "No more, no more," so can you.

Now that you know about the physical and psychological components of your internal success system, the next stop on your success journey of getting from **"here to there"** is discovering where the **"here"** is. The power of self-awareness awaits.

Chapter Three

THE POWER OF SELF-AWARENESS

"The map is not always the territory"
Anthony Robbins

Getting from here to there begins with understanding where **here** is on your volleyball map. It's called self-awareness. Even with a road map in your hands, you can't intelligently ask for directions to anywhere unless you first know where **here** is. The same strategy applies to your volleyball journey. You need to know **where you are** before you can move in the direction of **where you want to go.** Without knowing what your strengths and weaknesses are, intelligent goal setting is difficult.

A complete and accurate inventory of your strong and weak skills and attitudes is a good start. But self-awareness truly begins by knowing the full potential of your inner resources, understanding the unlimited power of your imagination, and, of course, acknowledging your greatest power, the power to choose the direction you want your life to take.

As you travel life's path, you need to be constantly alert to the impact the **pain and pleasure principle** has on its traveling companions, your self-image and comfort zone. There are no forces more powerful in determining your ultimate destination than your two basic needs of **avoiding pain and gaining pleasure.** When you make most of your on-court decisions based on the need to avoid pain, both your self-image and comfort zone suffer excessive damage. Then the trouble begins. When your unsure self-image and small comfort zone realize that you're dreaming of an exciting journey, your inner voice may respond, **"It's too tough! I can't do this! I'm tired, give it a rest! Think of the embarrassment if I mess it up!"**

A Self Image Check

The problem with traveling with an out-of-control, poor self-image and a small comfort zone is that every time you have a tough decision to make on the court, the tendency is to lower your goals and expectations. Your game strategy is to do what you do best and take the safest route. Fear of failure and a feeling of unworthiness cause you to avoid those same weak skills you should be developing into strengths. You take few chances and, as a result, experience little change in your game.

You already know the good news. Since the self-image is your creation, freeing yourself from the bondage of a disempowering self-image can be your doing, too. Your human computer operates on the same principle as all mechanical computers function – **input determines output.** The task of expanding your self-image and comfort zone requires a great deal of positive thinking and doing. But first, let's examine your old way of thinking and doing so that you'll know exactly what you'll need to change.

This means being totally honest with your game and evaluating what you do well and what you don't with no exaggerations or deceptions. Promise us that after you identify those weaknesses, you'll refuse to accept them as permanent, but rather as creative opportunities that will help you dramatically improve your game.

A Question Of Degree

Once you understand that all skills, attitudes, and emotions are neither good nor bad but simply in various stages of growth and development, your self-image will experience an immediate lift. There's a tendency in most athletes and coaches, especially when the self-image is soft, to see things in black and white – good or bad. In reality, there are degrees of effectiveness.

Shakespeare said, **"Nothing is either good or bad, but thinking makes it so."** That is solid advice worth considering now that you don't have to accept your weaknesses as permanent. What Shakespeare failed to mention was that changing the way you think can effectively be accomplished in small degrees!

An itemized list of your volleyball assets with an attached degree of proficiency can help you establish exactly where you are as a player. Then you'll not only have a detailed map to accurately follow on your volleyball journey, you'll also know the territory that must be traveled.

A realistic inventory of your current skills and attitudes will give you a clear picture of every one of your self-images. The psychological fact is that each one of your volleyball skills has its very own self-image mirroring it. For example, if you see yourself as a defensive specialist who rarely registers a kill from the front row, you'll probably find a reason not to take advantage of that great set. In reality, what's holding you back is a fear of failure produced by a soft self-image. No matter how hard you practice aggressive attacking, unless you **see yourself** swinging quickly and scoring the kill, the skill development won't stick! It's not how well you can hit the ball; it's how clearly you **see yourself** swinging and scoring the kill that is important.

Now, are you ready to look within from above? You'll find the view quite revealing.

A Self-Awareness Inventory: Looking Within From Above

Let's begin your self-evaluation on the defensive side of the ball. Here is a list of defensive traits for self-appraisal. Score yourself using a scale of 1-10. A score of 1 represents a low self-estimation; a 10 signifies an extraordinary, super skill or attitude level. A score of 5 stands for a playable but not consistent skill; an 8 for a "ready for prime time skill."

In order to objectively increase your self-awareness level, use the following visualization procedure. Observe yourself competing from an aerial view. Normally you evaluate yourself and the world from an inside-out perspective. With an **outside-in look,** you'll be able to judge your performance less personally.

Do this: Visualize yourself leaving your body and feel yourself rising up to the ceiling. Now, imagine yourself looking down, but instead of seeing yourself reading this book, you have a bird's eye view of a volleyball court on which two teams are playing a hotly contested game. Zero in on the game. There you are right in the middle of the action doing your thing. You're watching yourself playing defense. Let's test all of your defensive self-images. Remember to rate (from a 1 to 10) each skill or attitude ability you see yourself performing.

Judge Your Defensive Ability To:

1. **Dig a hard driven spike...** Are you anticipating the angle at which the offensive player is attacking? Are you moving your feet quickly enough to position your body in line with the incoming ball? Are you digging the spike? _____

2. **Set the block...** Are you setting the block in the right position? _____

3. **Be aggressive...** Are you forceful and physical? _____

4. **Compete with intensity...** Are you maintaining a high degree of desire? _____

5. **Play with courage...** Can you see yourself sprawling to save a ball, digging a ball out of the net, or sacrificing your body for your team? _____

6. **Enjoy playing defense...** Do you see yourself excited, enthused, and having fun? _____

7. **Make a big defensive play...** Do you see yourself turning a game around by making a key dig, save, or block? _____

8. **Read and move...** Can you see yourself actively reading the attack and moving to the area in your zone where the ball will most likely be sent? Are you a positive part of the "Team Defense"? _____

9. **Play at the net...** Are you playing big? _____

10. **Stay Strong...** How's your endurance? _____

The purpose of this test is to open an avenue of communication between you and your many self-images. Notice that some of your self-images are stronger than others. Later on, using the power of visualization, we'll show you how to increase your score, inch by inch. At the same time you'll have an opportunity to reshape the controlling self-image.

JUDGE YOUR OFFENSIVE ABILITY TO:

For now, let's go back to the same aerial view and evaluate your skills and attitudes on the offensive end of the court using the same 1-10 scale:

1. **Hit the hard-driven spike** _____

2. **Hit the ball around the block** _____

3. **Create an off-speed shot or tip for yourself with a decisive move** _____

4. **Set the errant pass if you're a hitter, so that your team can get off an attack** _____
   or set any pass if you're a setter, where your hitter can get a good swing _____

5. **Move in transition from "D" to "O"** _____

6. **Handle the ball (set and pass)** _____

7. **Serve** _____

8. **Make the first pass** _____

JUDGE YOUR CHARACTER:

A final aerial look at your inner character and attitudes (1 to 10):

1. **Sportsmanship** _____

2. **Performance in the clutch** _____

3. **Determination** _____

4. **Rapport with teammates** _____

5. **Rapport with coaching staff** _____

6. **Optimism** _____

7. **Positive self-talk** _____

8. **Ability to set realistic goals and achieve them** _____

9. **Honesty and integrity** _____

10. **Self-confidence** _____

11. **Concentration (pinpoint and peripheral)** _____

12. **Composure (control your emotions)** _____

13. **Competitiveness** _____

14. **Contribution to the team** _____

15. **Perseverance** _____

16. **Commitment** _____

17. **Courage** _____

18. **Ability to take on a challenge or risk** _____

19. **Resiliency** _____

20. **Ability to handle frustration** _____

This final visualization session will not be easy. Evaluating your attitude and character may require several tries. Recalling specific situations can help. Judge the inner skills and character you displayed and grade yourself accordingly. With time and practice, you'll get better at this numbers game.

SCORE THE EVENTS OF THE DAY

Sharpen your self-awareness ability at the end of each day by looking back at certain events that happened that day in practice, the match, or the locker room. Close your eyes, recall the aerial view, peer down and numerically grade your response in those recently experienced situations (1-10). Before falling asleep at night is a good time to run these events through the mirror of your mind and score yourself. The habit of reviewing your daily performance and grading these events will help you make more profitable decisions in the future.

After matches, feel free to update your inventory scores. Each time you do, you will be telling your self-image that you are aware it's expanding and improving **inch by inch** and that you appreciate even the smallest change. Not only will **knowing thyself** "inch by inch" make you a better player, you'll be a better person too!

Avoid The #10

Athletes coach themselves the way coaches coach. They correct to perfect. There's no easier way to abuse the self-image than to strive for perfection. Don't get caught in the pressure trap of having to attain a "10" in order to feel good about yourself. Volleyball is not a game of perfection. If you're thinking you've got to be perfect to win, very few things you do on the court will be fun. In time, the only thing you'll achieve is **burnout.** We worry for a coach who says his team must play a **perfect** game in order to win. The pressure to play well is too immense. Those teams rarely win the big ones.

Valuable Self-Image Insights

If you're not satisfied with the outcome of your performance inventory, you've got two choices: to **fix the blame or to fix the problem.** The easy way is to blame your genetic make-up (grandfather was a hothead, too). However, if you want to be in charge of your personal remote control system, show some resourcefulness. Here are some self-image insights:

1. Realize that low self-description is self-defeating and puts a lid on your potential. "That's my nature, that's me. I can't help it," is unacceptable and prevents you from taking responsibility for your life.

2. Understand that all negative *I am's* can be traced to the poor self-image which you have created.

3. Before falling asleep, make it a habit to remind yourself of the positive contributions you made during the day.

4. Realize you have only winning skills and attitudes. However, know that some are in a stage of early development. Skills are never finished products. With a commitment to change, your skills will improve. Be patient and persistent.

5. As long as you continue to label yourself clumsy, you will have a built-in reason to be a loser.

6. Eliminate the *I am's* that are negative and create positive *I am's*. *I'll try,* is unacceptable because it's a comfort zone effort (losers try). *I'm enthusiastic, I'm aggressive, I'm capable,* are the basis for new self-talk conversations.

7. Understand that there is joy in a new way of thinking and doing. Not only does success come in *can's,* so does happiness.

8. It's time to realize that the power and freedom to choose which attitudes you want is in your hands, or should we say your head. What you do with this power is totally up to you. It's your responsibility, so decide now to respond with ability!

Why You Must Value Yourself

There has never been another person exactly like you, and there never will be! When you consider your uniqueness, it's impossible to demean yourself.

You have been gifted with a miracle producing **Internal Success System** and the freedom to choose how to use it. Find your real purpose and you will have more than you need to live an exciting and rewarding life. Maybe the philosopher was right when he said, **"Life's purpose is to find a purpose."** Is playing winning volleyball yours? Only you can make that decision. Whether it is or isn't, we can tell you this: **The lessons you learn along your volleyball journey will help you develop the winning strategies and beliefs you'll need when you do find life's real purpose. Maybe that is why you are playing volleyball.**

Value Your Teammates

You must accept and appreciate the uniqueness of your teammates, managers, and coaches. They have been gifted with the same **Internal Success System** and power to choose as you have. The belief and value systems of others are usually different, but team goals must be unified if a successful season is to be expected.

It is not necessary that every player on the team is likable. What is important is that everybody on the team understands and likes one another. If you want to like someone, try looking for the good. Do you look for the good in your teammates and others you meet? You should. By looking for the good in others you find the good in yourself. The opposite is also true. Look for the bad in others and you expose the bad in yourself.

There is a **looking-for-the-good** game that Stan plays at airport terminals that is lots of fun. While waiting for a flight, he sits and watches people pass and makes it a game to identify one unique and likeable quality each of them has. It can be anything from the purposeful way they carry themselves, the uniqueness of their clothes, or some positive characteristic of their physical appearance. The game does more than pass the time of day, it puts him in an optimistic frame of mind for travel and living.

Team Bonding

Here's a **looking-for-the-good** exercise your team can play after workouts on the floor or in the locker room after matches. It's called the **Circle for Giving and Forgiving** or the **Attitude of Gratitude Circle.** We have a lot of fun with it at camp, and it really helps the players appreciate, respect, and bond with their teammates. The team circles up as each player takes a turn recognizing a positive contribution that the teammate standing to his/her right made during the game. Even if a player didn't play well or didn't play at all, you can always find something good if you sincerely look for it.

A great waste of energy is focusing on what is wrong. Conversely, there is a synergistic benefit when all players on a team develop the habit of valuing each other. Remember this: Look for wrong and you'll find wrong. Look for good and you'll find good. Find good and you'll feel good. You decide which direction empowers you the most.

THE CHOICE IS YOURS

In closing we hope you'll be more alert to your greatest power —your freedom to choose which goals excite you the most and in the long run will bring you the most happiness. Appreciate your personal power to choose to be....

goal oriented or aimless	**alert or unobserving**
a "now person" or procrastinator	**aggressive or timid**
courageous or fearful	**determined or a quitter**
a worker or idler	**enthusiastic or indifferent**
creative or mechanical	**a giver or taker**
relaxed or uptight	**a winner or loser**

This can be your ultimate awareness — the power to choose how you want to utilize your **Inner Success System.** With this thought in mind, let's examine the how-to process for fully activating your **Internal Success System** for the volleyball success you desire. It's time to discover the **Ultimate Success Formula of Volleyball Cybernetics** and learn exactly how you can live your dream.

PART TWO

The Ultimate Success Formula

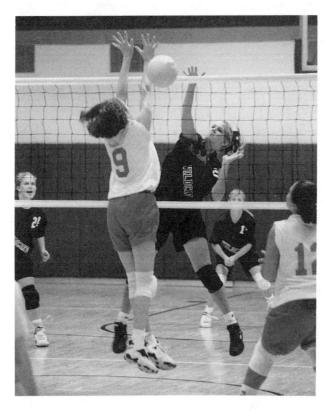

*"We are what we repeatedly do.
Excellence, then, is not an act but a habit."*
Aristotle

F.A.S.T.: THE ULTIMATE SUCCESS FORMULA

"From the lowliest depth there is a path to the loftiest height."
Carlyle

Winners have a strategy worth remembering. It's called **WIT, "Whatever It Takes."** Achievers always seem to find a way to get the job done no matter what the adversity. This is the **WIT** part of the process. By using the acronym **FAST**, our success formula will be clearly laid out in the correct sequence.

Find a goal and a reason why you must achieve the goal.
Find a compelling reason and sticking to your game plan for success will be possible.

Act as if
Learn how to model the winner's body language and self-talk. It's the fastest way to condition your **Internal Success System** to produce winning skills and attitudes.

See what you want
Winners have a habit of **seeing** what they want. Losers tend to **see** what they want to avoid. Get smart and fully use the great power of mental visualization to develop beliefs that empower your game.

Take action until...
Stay persistent until you get what you want.

Chapter Four

FIND A GOAL... AND A REASON TO WANT IT

"If the why is big enough, the how-to will come."
Anthony Robbins

Cybernetics is a Greek word meaning the steersman. Goals provide direction, therefore goal setting is the first step in the "doing" process. Your success mechanism is constructed so that it automatically steers you in the direction of your goal.

Accomplishing your goal is another matter and does not always happen right away. That's why it's crucial to ask yourself, "Is achieving this goal important to me?" Without a compelling reason **why you want what you want,** perseverance won't be the name of your game. Reasons come before results. Establish a reason why you want to develop a certain skill or attitude. Strong signals will be sent to your subconscious, telling your habitmaker you are not satisfied with the way things are, and that your control center is demanding a change, right now!

Here is an example of the importance of first finding a powerful reason before you can achieve a goal. At camp we ask the athletes to challenge themselves to see how many times in a row they can perform a certain skill correctly. They can perform the skill by themselves and/or with a partner. The rule is they can only work on this "consecutive best" challenge during free time. At the end of the camp day those athletes who attained the top scores in consecutive serving, setting, and passing both as individuals and pairs are rewarded in some small way. As the camp week progresses fewer and fewer campers take on the challenge. Why did most lose interest? We asked those who stayed with the challenge why they decided to spend all of their free time monotonously passing or setting a volleyball back and forth. The response is always the same. It was not the prize, nor was it the skill improvement that motivated them. They simply loved the challenge. They wanted to see how many times they could do it in a row. What a simple but pure reason. There were campers who spent hours partner passing or setting over 1,000 consecutive times without a mishap, just because they wanted to see if they could do it! Can you believe that?

For the winner, loving the challenge is more than enough. What is your reason for wanting what you want? More playing time? Want to make a greater contribution to your team? Is it for the glory, the love of the challenge, or simply to see how good a competitor you can be? Find a big enough reason why and the power will be there. Count on it!

Dave's team did exactly that a few seasons back. Dave had a strong team returning whose main goal was to defend the conference co-championship won the previous year. Their preseason scrimmages, however, were unimpressive. After winning their opener they faced one of the biggest challenges of the season, their arch rival who had shared the crown with them. Dave will always fondly remember what happened that night. The Wildcats rallied to win game one, then romped in game two with the capacity crowd going wild! Dave's girls played that night at a level they had never reached before. Even though they would go on to finish 21-2, win the conference, and advance further in the tournament than any other team in the school's history, they never again put it together like they did that magical night.

While being interviewed after the game, Jodi, the team's captain explained, "We really wanted this game because we were very disappointed that we ended up co-champs with them last year. We felt we were better and we had to prove it to ourselves. Tonight we did!" Dave's team found a reason to want that match more than any other that season. So they went out and got it!

MAKE SURE YOUR GOALS ARE REALISTIC

Setting realistic but challenging goals can be a problem. With a poor self-image leading the way, you could be heading for a big fall.

Dave recalls a camper by the name of Sarah whose unrealistic goal was to be an Olympic player. Sarah was slower than slow and as if this wasn't enough of a handicap, she had a bad habit of not completing even simple plays during camp games. She often "dead-ended" the play with a missed spike, a bad pass, or a net foul. Without a realistic self-image, Sarah created a fictitious self. She covered up an insecure self-image by setting unreachable goals for herself. Because she had to impress others, she became a "hot dog" on the court. She would make easy plays look difficult. Many of her mistakes were the result of an overtrying effort. Dave never told her that making the Olympics was out of the question. What Dave did do was encourage her to set some immediate self-improvement goals that could help her contribute to her team's success at camp. Sarah was asked to accomplish the little things at first: like being able to get her body behind the ball, making a good pass to the setter at a key moment, and especially not trying so hard when serving at a crucial point of the match.

We all have a freedom to choose goals that are best for ourselves, but most of us do tend to underestimate our ability to reach for goals that we are capable of achieving. William James, the father of modern psychology estimated we use only ten percent of our natural mind capacity.

He probably overestimated. Recent estimates state that less than four percent of our mind potential is actually tapped. More often than not, coaches of all sports know that there are too many athletes on their teams that have never come close to realizing their true talents.

HOW TO USE YOUR INVENTORY TO ESTABLISH SMART GOALS

There is power in self-awareness because it tells you what you need. Use the results from the self-awareness test to set some realistic and challenging goals for yourself.

For a start, select one skill that you feel will improve your game the most. Is it the ability to "hit around the block"? Let's say you gave yourself a rating of 5 on the inventory. Close your eyes and focus in on the number 5 for a few seconds. Now mentally increase that number by two points. Hold that image of 7 in your mind's eye for at least thirty seconds. You have now determined a specific and very reachable skill goal for your subconscious to act upon. Your mission is to improve your ability to hit "around the block" to a 7 level. Now think, "What will I have to do on the court to increase my performance level for hitting 'around the block' by two more points? How much better will I have to swing to attain the higher score?" If you can't answer that question accurately, this will help. Is there someone on your team who has a 7 level skill for hitting "around the block"? In Chapter 6, **Seeing What You Want,** we'll show you how to visualize and model that better hitter inch by inch and achieve a higher score for yourself. But for now, let's continue to "goal-shop" for your subconscious. Do this:

1. Select two more skills from offense and defense and two important attitude habits.
2. Mentally establish a score of two points higher for each skill and attitude.

Follow our goal-setting guidelines and enjoy the tremendous power goals provide.

1. Set goals that are high enough so that they present a challenge, but are within reach.
2. A goal must be one that can be conceptualized, mentally seen in the mind's eye as a **goal-picture** or **end-result** picture. You must believe there is a real possibility that the goal can be reached. If the goal cannot be conceptualized by you, it will not be realized. It was only after Roger Bannister became the first runner in history to run a sub-four minute mile that other outstanding milers were suddenly able to achieve the same feat, because those talented runners could finally conceptualize a successful sub-four minute mile!
3. Goal cards: You must constantly remind yourself of your goals. Write them down in a one, two, or three-word expression that creates a clear and positive **word-picture** of what you want. Any 3 x 5 index cards will do. Duplicate the cards. Put them in places where you can't avoid seeing them, for example, the wall of your bedroom, on the bathroom mirror, inside the cover of your notebook, on your desk, or inside your school locker.
4. Sign the cards on the bottom line as if they were a contract. They are!

   Consider it a personal commitment to the most important person you know in your life...yourself.

5. Write these two words on the top line of the cards: **I Can!**

6. Fix a deadline next to the goal. This is the date you expect to achieve this goal. Deadlines are excellent motivators because they offer the subconscious a specific time line instruction.

7. The goal must be something you want, not something that is imposed on you by your coach, friends, or family. The goal will lead to fulfillment of your own ambitions, not someone else's. The best way to determine if you really want the goal is to ask yourself these two empowering questions:

What will I gain if I achieve this goal?

What will I lose if I don't take action to achieve this goal?

Honestly answer these two **pain and pleasure** questions, and you'll have all the firepower you need to move toward, not away, from living your goal.

8. Establish one set of related goals at a time. Athletes who vacillate between goals or are constantly changing goals seldom achieve any of their goals. Dropping goals and selecting new ones means learning how to quit. Careful judgements must be made to see if a goal is truly attainable. If not, only then should a new goal be substituted.

9. Goals should not be destructive in nature. The goal should not harm, intimidate, or take advantage of another. Wanting to physically or mentally hurt someone or wish someone ill is wrong. These goals can be achieved, but you are using the marvelous power of your **Internal Success System** for the wrong reasons. Hurting or using someone will never bring you the lasting happiness you want. Never!

The most powerful electronic computer in the world has no power at all unless it's plugged into a goal. Winning starts at the beginning. So plug in to those goals that best meet your needs and your mental computer will have all the power it requires.

"EXCUSE ME GENTLEMEN! I THINK YOU'VE OVERLOOKED AN IMPORTANT FACTOR."

Ready for the second step in the **Cybernetics Success Formula?** Up next...how to develop that same feeling of certainty that the winner has by playing the game, **"Act As If."**

Chapter Five

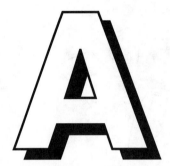

ACTING AS IF: MODELING THE BEST

"If you have no virtue, act as if."
Shakespeare

There is incredible power in **"acting as if"** you are a confident, aggressive, and poised volleyball player. You already know this works from your childhood days of playing **"let's pretend"** when you became what you were not. What you may not realize is that playing the game of **"acting as if"** offers one of the quickest, most reliable inner-game strategies to improve the self-image, expand the comfort zone, and control the focus of the **RAS. When you physically pretend to be what you are not, and you do it with conviction, your subconscious has no other choice but to grasp and act upon what you want.**

A COACH DISCOVERS THE POWER OF "ACTING AS IF"

After a disappointing tournament Coach Marty Petersen of the University of Wisconsin at Oshkosh was at a loss as to why her talented Titans were playing so inconsistently. Although they were 16-9 during the early part of the 1994 season, the coach was not satisfied with her team's performance. She explained, "We were losing matches which we had no business losing and our winning matches were an ugly sight to see. We had a ton of offense but our serving and passing limited our best hits to warm-ups." The frustrated coach couldn't understand how her team was passing and serving so poorly, especially when they were spending so much time working long hours on those skills during practice. A coaching friend suggested she try a different approach to solving the problem. "Start **acting as if!** No matter how poorly they are really doing, start telling your players they are getting better," was the friend's advice. Coach Petersen's immediate response was, "You've got to be kidding!" But with no other suggestions on how to get her team untracked, she decided to give the inner game idea a try.

Before their next practice the coach instructed her assistants that during all passing and serving drills they were to tell the players they were improving even if they weren't. For the next three days, the coaches stuck with their **act as if** plan. Surprisingly, by the end of the third day their passing and serving started to noticeably improve. Coach Petersen reasoned that the exaggerated praise allowed her players to stop worrying about making mistakes and "just get back to playing good volleyball." As the players' subconscious accepted the coaches' manufactured compliments as authentic statements of their true ability, an on-the-court success story was being created.

Inspired by the team's improvement as a result of the **acting as if** method, Coach Petersen sought out additional advice on mental training techniques. Soon she added daily relaxation, visualization, and affirmation exercises during practices and matches. As the players' confidence level continued to grow in leaps and bounds, so did their level of play. Marty Petersen's Titans didn't lose another match until they fell to Washington University of St. Louis in the Division III National Championship match. "I give a lot of the credit to the mental exercises we did. **Acting as if** certainly had a snowballing effect on my team," the happy coach concluded.

Are we suggesting that if you pretend to be intense, energized, and confident, in time you will develop these winning virtues? **No, not in time, but immediately! We are telling you that the transformation from "frog into prince or princess" can happen overnight! We remind you, again, that your subconscious absolutely cannot tell the difference between a real experience and one that is vividly imagined.**

THE POWER OF BODY LANGUAGE

When you change the physiology of your body, you change your state of mind. Change your state of mind and you change the direction of your playing destiny. The fact is that the way you move your body, express facial muscles, and even breathe are all linked to the way you feel, think, and perform. If you don't believe it, do this:

Stand up straight, throw your shoulders back, head up, and take several deep breaths.
With your eyes looking upward, put a great, big smile on your face and rapidly slap your hands together
at least six times. With each powerful clap shout the word, "GREAT!"

Now, how do you feel? Feel any different than you felt before? If you did exactly as we suggested, you should feel more excited, energized, and powerful. **Your motion created emotion,** thanks to the body signals you sent to your subconscious. You can create any state of mind you want by controlling your body motion, breathing, facial expression, and even the tone of your voice.

Want to increase your confidence level right now? Follow these instructions and see what happens to the way you feel.

Can you remember a game or a part of a game in which you played flawlessly? Can you remember how you felt? You felt strong, decisive, and confident. You were unstoppable. Now stand up and move your body with the same excitement and assurance that you had in that game. Look the way you looked then. Put the same unbeatable expression on your face that you had then. Breathe deep and strong exactly the way you breathed then. Can you remember what you said to yourself or how you said it? Speak to yourself using the same tone of voice and the same feeling of certainty.

How do you feel inside? You should be feeling more confident, upbeat, and optimistic. When you duplicated the body language experienced during the past moment of greatness, you also duplicated the same confident state of mind. They are permanently linked and stored together in your mental computer.

MODELING THE BEST

Do you want to play more aggressively and with more decisiveness? Most athletes do. Whenever you mirror or copy someone's body language, self-talk, and thinking habits, the process is called **Modeling.** The procedure works this way:

- Identify someone who is aggressive.
- Duplicate the role model's strong, forceful habit of moving his or her body.
- Copy the model's intense facial expressions and deep breathing rhythm.
- Imagine what he or she is thinking.

Now you have a proven recipe for becoming an aggressive and forceful player.

CHANGING STATES IMMEDIATELY

The **Call-Off** and the **Growl-Off** are two techniques we use at camp to encourage athletes to play with more freedom, intensity, decisiveness, and aggressiveness. This is how it is done:

- A proven aggressive player volunteers to play the role of the model.
- Another volunteer, someone who wants to play with more aggressiveness, steps up.
- The two athletes face off with one another in front of the other campers.
- The aggressive player crouches down in a wide stance, back straight, elbows in, arms extended outward, in front and away from the body. Hands are below the waist, palms facing in. The role model puts on the most aggressive, intense facial expression and begins to loudly call for an imaginary ball, over and over again. Shouting, **"Mine! Mine! Mine!"**
- The less aggressive player is told to carefully study the performance of the role model and when he/she feels ready, to physically mirror the intense actions of the aggressive player. Using the same intensity, the unaggressive player must copy everything he or she sees, especially the strong tone when shouting, **"Mine! Mine! Mine!"**
- The fun begins when everybody in the gym matches up with a partner, including the coaches, and tries to out shout each other.

The "Growl-Off"

The **Growl-Off** game is the same except the role model growls and grunts at the top of his or her voice. The role model with the unlimited comfort zone is told to wildly contort the face, extend the hands above the armpits like a set of tiger claws, and jump wildly up and down screaming out the longest, loudest growl ever heard. You won't believe the intensity and noise in the gym when the players pair-up and try to outdo each other in volume and creativity. You can just hear their small comfort zones breaking up. The competition increases during an elimination tournament to find the meanest and best growler in the gym.

You may not believe that aggressiveness and intensity can be developed immediately, but you'll think differently after a couple of uninhibited **Call-Off!** and **Growl-Off!** competitions against your best buddy.

VIDEOTAPE MODELING

Another effective modeling method is to study and then mirror the actions of winners by watching videos of their best performances. This modeling technique is described by sports psychologist Martin Gipson and coaches Steve Lowe and Tom McKenzie in Carl McGowan's excellent book, **The Science of Coaching Volleyball.** They write that "modeling" is used extensively by the Women's National Team. Whenever a player is having a problem performing a certain skill, the coaches put together a videotape of that same player performing the skill correctly in both practices and matches. Every third skill demonstration is shown in slow motion to make it even easier for the player to see and feel herself performing the skill correctly. While watching the tape, the player is encouraged to verbally describe the part of the play she feels is most important to see.

This helps the athlete to focus on the key element of the play she most needs to improve. The video tape watching is repeated three times a week as a supplement to the on-the-court training being done to correct the problem. This method is used not only with physical skill problems, but also with players who are having a **confidence crisis.** The coaches discover that when players simply look at themselves performing at the top of their game, they can immediately recapture that **winning feeling** once more.

JUST LOOK AROUND

There are unlimited resources where you can apply your mirroring process. Just keep your eyes open. Dave remembers a young player at his middle school camp years ago. The girl, going into the ninth grade, was one of the top players at camp. During camp a guest speaker was brought in to talk to the girls about what they needed to do in high school in preparation to play college volleyball. The speaker was Rebecca Yarish, who had previously won the area's top high school award as Miss Volleyball and was currently the star middle hitter for Kent State. At the conclusion of her talk, the campers asked Rebecca to spike a few balls. You can imagine how the sight of a six foot middle hitter pounding the ball to the floor excited the campers. At the end of the demonstration the young player went over to her high school coach, who was working the camp, and emphatically told her that she wanted to hit like Rebecca did. She even went on record by telling her coach that she flat-out wanted to hit like Rebecca, "Right now!" Greta Johnson, that aspiring young athlete in Dave's middle school camp, became an outstanding middle hitter for the University of Akron.

A DETERMINED ATHLETE STUDIES THE BEST

Diane Diglio was a 14 year old who loved to play softball. So much so that she became the hard hitting, slick fielding first baseman for the Carle Place Junior Varsity Softball Team on Long Island. Hitting .536 with an extraordinary on-base percentage of .741 and 24 runs batted in in only 15 games, you wouldn't know there was anything different about this 5 foot 9 inch softball star. But there was. Diane's right arm, malformed at birth, was missing a hand. Her right arm ended just below the elbow.

She loved to watch her brother Anthony play baseball. She dreamed of playing, too, but she couldn't catch and throw in one seamless effort. That was until she watched the 1988 Summer Olympics in Seoul, South Korea on TV. She was six years old at the time and as she watched a baseball game, a light bulb went on in her head. Jim Abbott, currently a Major League pitcher, who had one arm malformed at birth was pitching and winning. What an awakening for Diane. If he could field and throw, she thought, so could she. "I saw him pitch the ball," Diane said. "Then so he could field he immediately switched his glove under his arm and onto his hand. When I saw him do that, I thought, 'Wow.' It's possible." Almost every day after she saw what Jim Abbott could do with the glove, Diane Diglio dedicated her efforts to being the best softball player she could be.

Who are your role models? Are they inspirational? Stop doubting and start modeling a winner. Listen to what Diane said about the many doubters in her life. "Although I thought it was unfair for people to doubt me, what is important is the person on the inside. All I know is that all the people who thought I couldn't play softball, now know I can." Credit the determination of one athlete and her inspirational role model.

THE MASTER MODELING TECHNIQUE OF CYBERNETICS: THE SCIENCE OF VAK

VAK is our key cybernetic master modeling technique for training your subconscious to produce winning skills and attitudes. All programming input that enters your mental computer from the external world is received from your five senses. What you see, hear, feel, smell, and taste all become feedback data. You'll work three of your major senses by playing a game called **"follow the winner"** to program more powerful feedback signals into your mental computer. By carefully studying the best as they perform, you'll have a proven and quick method for skill and attitude development.

VAK is the acronym the science of Neuro-Linguistic Programming created to explain the modeling process. The three senses you'll employ are **V** for visual or sight, **A** for auditory or hearing, and **K** for kinesthetic or feeling.

V for Visual: Your subconscious prefers pictures. Before you can mirror a winner's performance strategy, you need to find out what the action you wish to duplicate looks like.

A for Auditory: Your subconscious listens to what you say to yourself. Involve the left side of your brain in the programming process. By employing words or sounds, you can elicit the winner's internal strategy. Words that take the form of self instructions and questions that empower allow you to lock into the same inner description of success that your role model experiences. Words like, Yes!...Great!...Stay Cool!...Relax!...Do It! or Slow Down! tend to produce the same conditioned responses that the winner produces. Questions like, "What have I learned?" and "What must I do so that this doesn't happen again?" should also be part of your auditory rap.

K for Kinesthetic: Your subconscious responds to your emotions and feelings. Last but not least, you need to experience the same emotions and feelings the winner experiences. You need to know what it "feels like" to execute a winning skill. Remember the effects of the "Call-Off!" and the "Growl-Off!"?

In order to probe the winner's exact internal and external strategy you must, first learn how to **"see it," "hear it,"** and **"feel it."** We'll get together in the gym to prove the power of **VAK,** first hand, but before we do, let's examine **the power of words.** Words have changed the destiny of nations and individuals. Words can also delight or devastate your playing destiny.

THE POWER OF POSITIVE SELF-TALK

Achievers do not talk to themselves in the same way underachievers do. Another action you can take to improve your game is to improve the quality and quantity of what you say to yourself. Upgrade what you say, how you say it, and how often you say it. Then self-talk becomes a breakthrough tool that quickly changes your state of mind.

Whenever you find yourself in a power state of mind, positive self-talk can help you lock in that feeling of success more permanently. By keeping the inner conversations positive, you tend to stay on course. Wallow in the garbage of negative self-talk, and your volleyball journey zig-zags with inconsistent play.

Words have started and ended wars, moved us to tears, made us laugh, solved our problems, and empowered us to live better lives on and off the court. It's time to shape your own performance destiny with the power of words. Do a little destiny shaping right now. Recite this: **"My serve is incredibly great and my talent is awesome!"** Say it several times more and make sure that you add as much passion and belief as possible into the way you recite this affirmation. Make it a habit to repeat this affirmation after you have made a great serve in practice or a game. Your subconscious will be listening and remembering.

HOW TO KILL A TREE... AND A DREAM

Have you heard the story about the witch doctor on a small island in the South Pacific who became famous for killing trees by yelling at them? When a tree grew too big that the natives were unable to cut it down with their primitive cutting implements, the witch doctor was brought in to do his thing. He had a strange method for downing a big tree. He would sneak up behind the tree at night, and for the next thirty days and nights, scream bloody murder at the tree. Although the witch doctor's technique was bizarre, he never failed to down a tree. The natives believed that by yelling at the tree, the witch doctor killed its spirit.

You may not believe the validity of this story, but should you find yourself shouting angrily at yourself long and hard enough, you're bound to kill the spirit of your own dream. It's a sad fact that the third leading killer of young people today is suicide. We bring up this subject of suicide not to depress you, but to impress upon you the power of negative self-talk.

There is a phenomenon called **partial suicide** of which you ought to be aware. Put yourself down after every mistake, and you'll be committing **partial suicide** by killing off your volleyball dream. **Partial suicide** means that your self-image and comfort zone shrink to the size where you're afraid to make a mistake or take a risk. You employ only the skills of which you're sure. Your favorite expressions become **"I can't,"** **"I won't,"** and **"I better not!"** And your volleyball dream is as dead as if the witch doctor worked you over for thirty days and nights!

POWER TALK

Do you know when you recite a key word while performing a certain skill, the word and the action are stored together? Literally anchored together and recorded, the word and action form a cybernetic loop in your brain. Here's the shocker. Recall the word to which the action is associated and the action is not only recalled, it's relived! Think of it. What a fast and easy way to train your subconscious to go into "rewind."

Take the action of spiking, for example. Shout the word **"Crush!"** at the exact moment you contact the ball, and two good things happen inside your mental computer.

1. The word **Crush!** and the spiking action form a cybernetic loop and are recorded (anchored) together.
2. The verbal left side of your brain is kept busy from overthinking or producing negative thoughts. Thus, the visual right side of the brain is free to do its thing of responding to sensory data needed to spike a volleyball.

Do you see the training advantages? You can program your subconscious with imaginary experiences of spiking a ball by simply reciting the word **Crush!** over and over again. Recite the word **Crush!** 50 times and your mental computer is simultaneously recording 50 successful kills. Recite the word **Crush!** while spiking and you will be developing the habit of clearing your mind of extraneous thoughts or doubts. By keeping your left brain busy with key **Power Words** like **Crush!** your brain will be unable to produce negative thoughts.

No, we are not asking you to recite a word each time you perform a certain skill in a game, but you can in drills. Later at your convenience program that skill by repeating the associated word 50 or more times. In time, not only will your skill level improve, you'll also find yourself doing more and thinking less in competition.

At camp, key words are connected to serving, spiking, passing, quickening feet, digging, blocking, and setting. Skills can then be programmed anywhere at any time: when resting, while watching television, eating meals, walking, or while turning the pages of this book.

POWER WORDS AND MODELING

Power Words can be applied to the modeling process. If your arm swing is not as quick and powerful as you want it to be, pay close attention to a teammate's decisive swing in practice. The moment your role model spikes the ball recite the word **Crush!** and imagine that it is you who is successfully spiking the ball. Do the **Power Word Modeling** for a week and judge your spiking ability. The results will be in exact proportion to the time and effort invested. "Repetition is the mother of skill," says Neuro-Linguistic guru Anthony Robbins. So stay with it.

OUR FAVORITE POWER WORDS

Here is a list of **Power Words** you can use for programming various skills and attitudes. Feel free to create your own. Recite the **Power Words** to yourself at the exact moment that you are executing the action or watching someone else performing the skill. During a break in the action make it a practice to repeat the word slowly and as often as time allows.

Ball! or Mine! .....Positioning yourself properly to pass an incoming ball

See! ....Seeing the entire floor; reading the play with peripheral vision concentration

Sight! ....Pinpointing concentration on the ball

Feel! ....Developing the confident sense of "feel" while serving

Yes! ....Locking in the "success sensation" after a successful serve or play

Clear! ....Eliminating frustration of a missed ball or any mistake

Stop! ....Stopping all negative talk

Crush! ....Swinging quickly through the ball while spiking

Soft! ....Relaxing the hands to improve ball control when setting

Big! ....Playing bigger and stronger at the net

Next! ....Moving on to your next task, assignment, or game situation without looking back

POWER QUESTIONS

Winners know how to ask themselves the right kind of questions — questions that empower them and keep them on track. Underachievers know how to develop feelings of inadequacy, dependency, and hopelessness by asking themselves the wrong questions.

Push the right keys to the most efficient and powerful computer in the world, your brain, and in seconds it responds. Ask your **Internal Computer** to provide you with the firepower to face any challenge, solve any problem, upgrade your energy level, or produce the know-how to live your dream, and watch it work its supernatural powers. By entering better questions into your biological computer, you immediately adjust your **Reticular Activating System** from focusing on the mediocre to focusing on the miraculous — from a setting of survival to a setting of success.

STUPID QUESTIONS TO AVOID

Don't catch yourself asking these questions:
- Why does it always happen to me?
- Why can't I get better?
- What's the use?
- Why is my serve so lousy?
- Why was I born so slow?
- Why do I always shank my passes?
- Why is life so unfair?
- Why is my talent so limited?
- Why is practice so boring?
- What else could I be doing if I weren't spending all this time practicing?
- When will this work?
- Why do my teammates (or coach) dislike me?
- When am I going to catch a break?

Your **Mental Computer** serves you faithfully, but remember it is impersonal to a fault. Ask it stupid questions and it produces stupid answers like **"that's the way it is and that's the way it will always be!"** Start now, by seeking more resourceful questions that bring out the best, not the worst, in your powerful **Mental Computer.** Stupid questions will keep you living inside a comfort zone that offers the illusion of security but little else. Every success story includes a struggle of some kind. Don't make your struggle permanent or personal by asking the wrong kind of questions. At one time or another, every successful athlete has stepped out from under a cloud of self-doubt. Doubt is good because it tests your resolve. Stupid questions are just plain dumb because they put your destiny into the hands of other people or other things. The next time you are confronted with a feeling of fear or unworthiness, a mistake, a tough call, a loss or a bad break, slow down and ask yourself empowering questions that bring out your best.

Need a state of mind or mood change after a discouraging setback? Try these winning questions on for size. One should fit the occasion.

- What have I learned?
- What must I do so this never happens again?
- How must I change so I get the results I want?
- What must I do to become totally committed?
- Whom do I know that I can go to for help?
- What must I do, today, to take action?
- What is the ultimate reward for my efforts?
- What is great about what I am doing?
- What is fun about what I am doing?

47

- How can I turn all this hard work into play?
- What am I excited about?
- What am I happy about?
- What valuable lesson did I learn?
- What did I do well in practice or the match?
- Whom have I helped today?
- What am I most grateful for today?
- What am I most proud of today?
- What can I do to improve the lives of my teammates and coaches?

By asking yourself these questions you are telling your fantastic **Focusing Device,** the **RAS,** to search out the good in others and yourself. Make it a habit to ask yourself two questions a day that can empower you to keep moving towards achieving your goal or training task. Stan's favorite questions are:

What am I going to accomplish today and have fun while I'm doing it?"

Then should anything go wrong, Stan immediately empowers himself with:

"What's good about it?"

PLAY "WHAT'S GOOD ABOUT IT" WITH YOUR TEAM

Master coaches get **master** results because they know how to help their players **master** their state of mind. These coaches understand that poor team workouts or shoddy match performances are not only part of the game, they are chock full of valuable "learning" messages.

Coach, with this in mind how about playing Stan's favorite game, "What's Good About It?" with your team after a mediocre practice or ragged game performance? This therapeutic process will lift player spirits and increase team optimism when events go awry. It won't hurt your own optimism level, either.

Do this immediately after a sad team performance. Gather your brooding squad and tell them that they are not leaving the locker room until they (as a team) can list at least ten solid benefits they can draw from their less than sparkling play. Listen to what they offer and observe what happens to their mood. Their responses may include:

1. Well, now we know what doesn't work!
2. If we don't "come to play" we won't "come to win"!
3. We realize that frustration controls our play and is the enemy!
4. We learned that we must trust each other more!
5. Overtrying doesn't work!
6. Undertrying doesn't work, either!
7. We know we won't play well unless we play as a team.

48

8. We realize that to play well we must be more aggressive!
9. We have to put more commitment, focus, and energy into practice if we want better results!
10. If we work together we can accomplish anything, including creating this fun list.

Haven't you noticed that successful players are able to maintain their most powerful state of mind in competition regardless of what happens on the court. Isn't this the difference between players who consistently succeed and players who don't? Winning athletes and their coaches control their most productive state of mind rather than allowing their state of mind to control them. They know it's not what happens to them that matters as much as how they handle what happens. They also know optimism empowers...pessimism disempowers.

Coach, unless you are into punishing your players after a poor performance, try empowering them with an attitude of optimism by playing "What's Good About It?" as often as needed. Once on the bus returning from a loss, Stan and his team thought of 55 "what's good about it" reasons after noticing a dead squirrel on the side of the road! Because of this empowering game, a solemn bus was soon full of positive energy and creative excitement.

The next time you hear a negative comment or are forced to do something you would rather not do, just ask yourself, "What's good about it?" Force yourself to look for reasons until you find ten good ones. Then notice how good you feel. With an attitude that these answers inspire, how could life be boring or frustrating for long?

PROGRAMMING WITH POWER AFFIRMATIONS

Although your mind thinks best in images, specifically selected words can create pictures that transmit feelings. Get ready for the power of affirmations. The following positive statements will motivate and prepare you for peak performance. Repeated daily, affirmations become the clear instructions your subconscious needs to achieve positive change.

The affirmation process will help you to keep a positive mindset whenever you need a motivational pickup. There'll be times when things go wrong or when negative thoughts and self-talk appear. By getting into the habit of silently repeating to yourself your favorite affirmation before or during a match, or practice, destructive self-talk is eliminated. You'll find yourself in that winning groove once again, with a strong motivation to achieve remarkable results in competition.

As you begin this verbal reconditioning procedure, consider yourself a computer programmer feeding a new software program called **Power Talk** into a top-of-the-line IBM computer. The data is in the form of specifically worded phrases that will direct your computer to produce a higher level of confidence, poise, and winning skills.

Before the new programming can take effect, expect the old mental programs to question the validity of the new input. With time the new information will override the old and you will start to experience positive change. The first sign that the new tapes are being played may be as subtle as feeling less frustrated after failing to complete a play or missing a serve. You may also find that you focus better and think more optimistically in competition. Within days you should expect the first on-the-court breakthrough. You will notice you're playing more aggressively, taking more chances, and executing shots you never tried before. Best of all, you'll be completing more plays.

If you like, add inspirational "Rocky" type music as you deliver the affirmations to yourself. A good idea is to record a series of affirmations on an audio cassette and play the tape back whenever you need inspiration. Feel free to create your own. Personalize it to represent a certain skill or attitude you want to develop. What is it you want improved? Is it softer hands to set a ball, a more accurate topspin serve, or an attitude of increased trust towards your teammates, coach, or yourself?

Here's a list of our favorite affirmations:

1. My serve is incredibly great and my talent is awesome.
2. The drive and purpose of the winner flows through my body.
3. There is no limit to my strength, power, and quickness. I have more than enough to win.
4. My potential is unlimited. I compete with the confidence of a champion play after play.
5. Nothing bothers me in the heat of competition. I am poised and cool and always in control of my actions and reactions.
6. I let go of all past limitations and mistakes. They are gone forever.
7. My enthusiasm in practice pays off, and each day I play better in every way.
8. My moves and reflexes are smooth, quick, and sure.
9. I am a winner each time I compete.
10. Overconcern and overtrying are unnecessary because I trust in the power of my subconscious.
11. I am free to take any risk to win.
12. I possess all the confidence, control, and concentration necessary to play my best.
13. My mind's energy is clearly focused in the here and now. Nothing distracts me from completing the play.
14. A positive expectation, that winning feeling, is always with me.
15. I have the power and courage to successfully play the game I have imagined.
16. I work harder, practice, and play smarter than my opponents. My quest is to be the best.
17. I am unstoppable. My spiking motion is quick and strong and I always finish with a kill.
18. I am invincible!
19. Yes! I can.
20. I do the thing that is hard to do and the power comes!

AN AFFIRMATION CHALLENGE

Do affirmations really work? Well, do prayers? We challenge you to find out. Complete this ten day affirmation test starting now. This is what you have to do. Fill in the blank with a skill you'd like to effectively execute play after play. Then in a sincere and commanding monotone repeat the following affirmation to yourself a total of 100 times each day for ten days. Observe what happens to your game. That is a grand total of 1000 times you'll inform your subconscious to instruct your body exactly what it is you want it to do.

Want to become an awesome **hitting, serving, spiking, passing, digging, blocking, or setting** star performing with machine-like consistency? While performing, emotional detachment is important, so in a cool monotone tell your subconscious what you want. Fill in the blank and just start reciting:

I AM A *spiking* MACHINE!

Any time or any place is good. Before or after you perform a skill, if time allows, is good, too. The more, the better. You'll hear more about this powerful affirmation later.

TEAM HUDDLING

Team Huddling pays big dividends. Your team can make it a point to quickly come together and say a power word after each dead ball (if state rules allow). For example, after an impressive kill the team meets in the middle and shouts **"Aaaaahh Kill!"** For a block the team could use the words **"Aaaaahh Roof"** (or "Big"). The Huddling should last only a few seconds with everyone using the same power words. The players can select the verbal leader who initiates the power word to be shouted.

Huddling is fun and easy when all is going well, but it has its greatest impact when momentum is on the other side of the net. This is when certain aggressive players must step up and motivate their teammates to reach within themselves for that something extra. By using a power anchor word to liven things up, a team has a better chance to regain a positive and confident state of mind. Try it and see.

Carolyn O'Keefe remembers the benefits Huddling provided her team during her junior year at Emporia State University in Kansas. She said, "We were playing a tough rival. A teammate, after making a tremendous dig remained there on the floor, face down. The unexpected great play had left her relishing the moment. Suddenly our impatient captain started yelling at her to get up by shouting... **'Up!Up!Up!'** while clapping her hands together three times. After the game we all laughed about our captain's new cheer. What happened next surprised everyone. In the next game we started using **'Up!Up!Up!'** whenever a mental pickup was needed. The cheer seemed to have the effect of pumping us up. The team believed it was no coincidence that some of our best play came after we shouted **'Up!Up!Up!'** and clapped."

HOW AN AFFIRMATION WORKED FOR STAN

In 1987 Stan ran his first and only marathon. The event took place in Paris, France, and in more ways than one, Stan will never forget that day. It dramatically reaffirmed his belief in the power of affirmations. Especially this one: "Do the thing that is hard to do and the power will come."

Let Stan tell the story in his own words. "I run almost every day, maybe three or four miles on a good day. Most days, a two-mile slow jog is the full extent of my run. I was visiting my daughter Carolyne in Paris, where she was studying art at the Sorbonne. We decided to enjoy an early morning jog together through the streets of Paris. We suddenly came upon several thousand runners who were preparing to embark on the world famous International Paris Marathon. Then we heard the starter's pistol and felt the rush of runners fly past us. It was here that I made my first mistake. I foolishly told my daughter that running a marathon had always been a dream of mine. She looked at me and said, 'It's time to live your dream, Dad. Let's do it!' She started to run along with the marathoners and I followed. Before I knew it, I was making the turn at the Arc de Triomphe with the rest of the runners and there I was, living my dream.

All went fairly well until the 15-mile mark. Then my dream became a nightmare. I hit the proverbial wall. The pain was so great I stopped. I was about to quit for good when I heard an inner voice say, **Do the thing that is hard to do and the power will come!** How many times had I used that same advice to motivate others? The words helped me to take a few steps. Soon I was talking to myself aloud, **Do the thing that is hard to do and the power will come!** Repeating it louder and louder, I found my pace increasing. The words seemed to be tapping a hidden energy source. After five hours and twenty minutes of pure anguish, I finished my first marathon. With the help of an affirmation, I had fulfilled an improbable dream.

But it was what happened at the finish line that truly surprised me. Along with my daughter, who had finished the race hours earlier, a grateful French marathon runner was also there to greet me. He gave me an enthusiastic hug, kissed me on the cheek, and said, **'Merci beaucoup..merci beaucoup.'** Realizing I was American, he explained in a strong French accent that he was about to quit the race at the 19-mile mark because of severe leg cramps when I passed him shouting, **'Do the thing that is hard to do...!'** He said he heard my words and started reciting them to himself in French, **'Faites la chose qui est difficile a faire!'** He added that without those words of advice, he would not have finished the marathon."

There's a lesson to be learned here. When life challenges you, don't give up. Instead of feeling sorry for yourself, employ the power of affirmations to help you fight through the tough time. It worked for Stan and for an appreciative Frenchman. It'll work for you, too.

Chapter Six

SEE WHAT YOU WANT

"My imagination makes my reality."
Walt Disney

During a 1993 interview for *Volleyball Magazine*, Nebraska University sophomore standout, Allison Weston, was asked her thoughts on her chances of someday being named Division I Player of the Year. "It's a few years off, but I can see it," she replied. The 1995 Asics/VOLLEYBALL NCAA Division I Player of the Year was Allison Weston.

AN ATHLETE CREATES A MIRACULOUS CHANGE

How many times have you said, "I'll believe it when I see it!" Nothing wrong with the practical approach of looking at things, unless you're not *seeing* enough playing time because your coach isn't *seeing* you getting the job done enough times on the court. Why not reverse the attitude of "I'll believe it when I see it" to "I'll see it when I believe it!" with the power of visualization. Then *see* what happens to your game.

Carrie Broomfield did just that. A dominant high school player, Carrie was plagued by inconsistency throughout her first two collegiate seasons at Nebraska Wesleyan University. She then dramatically improved her game to a higher level by deciding to look within and believe in herself first. Let Carrie tell you about her junior year transformation in her own words.

"I had worked my rear off during the off season and headed into the season as strong as I've ever been. Competition for starting positions was fierce. At first I loved the challenge of constantly being pushed to play my best, but as the season went on I found myself getting less and less floor time. Coach stressed the importance of the bench player, but being a competitor I also knew that

I had the athletic ability to be one of the best on the floor. Somewhere along the way I had lost most of my intensity and confidence. I felt sure that if I could regain that fire I could earn some playing time.

At the time Coach (Wick) Colchagoff was always pushing the mental stuff he had learned at the **"Yes, I Can!" Camp.** Periodically during the season the team went through some mental imagery and self-affirmation exercises. I realized that if I was going to make a contribution something had to quickly change. My decision was to make a commitment to the mental game (which I hadn't done before). With nothing to lose and a starting position to gain, I began to imagine myself making the perfect play over and over again in my head every night before I went to bed. In matches as I waited for the serve I would imagine the ball coming to me and then I would see myself making the perfect pass or kill.

Almost overnight, I started believing in myself like never before. It was incredible how much more confidence and positive energy I had. I was becoming a force on the floor. There were times after a match I couldn't believe how well I played. Every time the ball was set to me, I just knew it was going down on the other side. My intensity on defense picked up 110%. I had the feeling that it was almost impossible for the other team to hit a ball at me that I couldn't dig.

Not only was I a starter, my new found optimism was affecting the play of others on the team. At the end of the season I was awarded all kinds of honors including All-Conference, All-Region, NAIA Player of The Week, and our team's Most Outstanding Offensive Player."

Was Carrie's miraculous change and her dedication to mental imagery just a coincidence? Check it out yourself and tell us what happens. In her senior year, Carrie led her team to a 23-12 season, the sweet 16, and a national ranking (8th). She also achieved third team All-American honors. Now you're about to discover the same inner game process Carrie used.

How To Paint Mental Pictures

How many windows are there on the front of your house? As you thought about an answer, did you see a mental picture of your house? The indisputable fact is that you think in pictures.

Because you think in pictures the power of your creative imagination will create your new playing future. Wasn't it those negative inner pictures supplied by your self-image that got your game into trouble in the first place? Since they are only pictures let's get rid of them! Once you replace them with more successful images, you'll notice new traits, attitudes, and skills appearing.

Positive Mental Picturing: The Key To Your Success Mechanism

It was Shakespeare who wrote, **"Assume a virtue if you have it not."** Was he aware that the subconscious cannot tell the difference between a real and imagined experience? You're going to assume new playing virtues by mentally picturing yourself completing plays. As far as your subconscious is concerned, these synthetic pictures will be the same as an on-the-court experience. The degree of sameness depends upon the vividness and detail of your mental pictures, and with a little practice, you'll get it right.

Don't tell us you can't visualize. You certainly can. Look at any object in the room and memorize it. Close your eyes and tell us its color. Describe its shape, size, and texture. See what we mean? We don't all visualize with the same degree of clarity. Mental visualization can range from a big, bright, clear, and colorful picture to just a feeling. With time and practice, visualization can become an emotional action sequence. Regardless of the size, scope, and intensity of your current inner movies, a subconscious effect is still registering.

The key to effective visualization for skill improvement is that you want your mental pictures to be as close to the actual experience as you can make them. You want to be able to actually **feel** the experience and incorporate these feelings into your brain's memory bank and nervous system. To become the volleyball player you'd like to be, you'll need to create a series of clear mental pictures and feelings of the skills you want to master. Hold these pictures long enough in your imagination, and your inner success system will have no choice but to accept them as true, especially when you begin to achieve results. The fundamental law of the mind is this: **Whatever you hold in your mind long enough grows and becomes real.** Think about those material things you've accumulated over the years which you consider valuable. Before you got them, didn't you think about them long and hard?

The best way to discipline your imagination is with multiple layers of positive images. By visualizing the exact images that you want for yourself over and over again, new mental microchips will be programmed and stored within the infinite capacity of your inner computer. It will be these recordings that instruct your subconscious mind to produce the conditioned responses called skills. No matter how brief a time you hold the mental pictures don't get discouraged. Eventually you'll be able to create and hold positive pictures as long as you want.

IMAGINATION: STRONGER THAN WILLPOWER

When willpower and imagination are in conflict, willpower rates a distant second. Want proof? Think about a skill weakness you have. For example, you have trouble defending against a short tip or digging a ball tipped over the block. We both know that no amount of willpower is going to get that ball up in the air unless you have stored more green light images than red.

THE POWER OF IMAGINED PICTURES

Here's a mental exercise that illustrates the influence imagined pictures have over the subconscious.

Close your eyes and mentally travel into your kitchen at home. Walk over to the refrigerator. As you open the door, you hear that little suction sound the seal makes as it lets go. Next you can feel the cold breeze from inside escaping. Now reach down to that drawer where the fruit is kept and without even looking, feel around until you find a lemon. Bring it out, close the drawer, and then the door. Hear that neat sound as the seal sucks the door shut. Now you are holding a lemon in your right hand. You can feel its coolness and waxy texture. You can see its bright yellow skin. Try squeezing it a little. Can you feel its firmness? Now bring the lemon up to your nose and smell it. There's that unique lemon aroma. Mentally set the lemon down and begin to slice it with a sharp knife. Watch as the lemon juice squirts out when you cut it in half. Next, put the knife down and bring the lemon slowly up to your mouth. Get ready! Open wide and, yes, you guessed it, take a big, deep bite into the lemon. Feel that tart, sour flavor explode in your mouth.

Did you have any reaction to the above visualization? Did your mouth begin to salivate? Did you make a face in anticipation of the bite? Do you realize that **there is no lemon in the room?** Chances are that your subconscious directed you to one of these reactions because it was convinced that **there was a lemon in the room!** You used **visualization** to trick your subconscious into believing that you were sucking on a sour lemon. Thanks to your creative imagination, you sent image signals to your subconscious. Instantly, your automatic robot told your salivary glands to get busy. Saliva was secreted to wash away the tart taste of the lemon juice... an example of the power of suggested pictures.

This is the same power of mental imagery that produces your weak skills. There is a mental videotape orchestrated by your self-image instructing your subconscious to tell your body to shank the pass, miss the serve, or allow your opponent to spike the ball past you at the net. Your reliable and impersonal subconscious has no recourse but to carry out the commands. Don't blame it! Your subconscious does not know how to say no! So start picturing what you want. Your subconscious will do the rest. Trust its power to turn mental pictures into power performances.

VISUALIZING: MORE THAN JUST IMAGINING

It has been said, **What you can conceive, your body can achieve.** It's very important that you visualize the positive thought rather than just imagining it. Visualizing means not just seeing it, but feeling it, using as many of the body's senses as possible. The roar of the crowd (sound), the glitter of the scoreboard (sight), and the texture of the ball (touch) are all factors that make the imagined experience acceptable instruction for your subconscious.

THE TWO VISUALIZATION PROCEDURES: ALPHA AND BETA

There are two kinds of visualization procedures that can help you train your mind. One is called Alpha programming, a deeper level of visualization, and Beta, the conscious level of visualization. Use either one and you upgrade your level of confidence.

The human brain actually radiates electrical impulse waves in different brain wave patterns. These waves can be measured by an EEG (Electroencephalograph). The rhythms of all mental energy are measured in cycles per second. When you're awake and active, your rhythm runs between 14 to 21 cycles per second. This state of mind is called the Beta level. A deeper level of mental activity is registered whenever a relaxed state of mind is achieved. The cycles per second drop between 7-14. This is called the Alpha level. This state can be attained naturally while you're lying comfortably in bed awaiting sleep or immediately after awakening in the morning. These are excellent times to visualize positive mental pictures since the subconscious at this deeper level of slow electrical activity is more susceptible to suggestion. The painting of mental pictures is more vivid, clearer, and detailed when the mind is uncluttered and free to work its charm with your success mechanism. Another good time for achieving the Alpha level is when you're sitting in a comfortable chair in a quiet room.

YOUR FIRST EXERCISE

Mentally visualize an official size volleyball with your eyes closed. To help you develop a more realistic picture of the ball, place an actual volleyball on your bed or desk in front of you before you start to visualize. Open and close your eyes until you can clearly see the volleyball with your eyes closed. As you visualize the ball on your inner mental screen (on the inside of your closed eyelids) repeat slowly to yourself, **"ball, ball, ball,"** for a minute.

The next step is to produce a picture of a net in your mind. Concentrate on the picture of the net until you can create the image on your mental screen with your eyes closed. Create the net in detail, color, and size. Repeat, **"over, over, over,"** silently to yourself.

YOUR FIRST ACTION MOVIE

Now combine the two visualizations (the ball and net) you have just created into one mental picture. Add motion to your visualization by **seeing** the ball fly over the net. Focus on this mental movie (see page 58) of the ball flying over the net until you can **feel** the ball clearing the net with your eyes closed. Replay your movie 50 consecutive times. Each time you mentally experience the successful sequence of the ball flying over the net, especially when **feeling** the action, your mind and nervous system are recording a successful serve. In fact, you've just completed 50 consecutive successful serves. Congratulations!

Once you develop clear and simple mental movies, it's time to graduate to more challenging and game-like movies. Are you ready to employ your greatest asset, your creative imagination, to turn any weak skill you choose into a strength? Let's see if *visual lies* can truly get your game out of first gear and into overdrive.

THE TRAINING PROCESS: CHANGING BELIEFS

It's no secret that mental visualization has provided athletes of all sports with a proven short-cut for attaining peak performance. Disciplining creative imagination is a powerful tool being used today to cure cancer, overcome stress, increase salesmanship, dissipate fears, conquer migraine headaches, high blood pressure, and obesity. Now it's your turn to take charge of your thoughts. By focusing on the same kind of beliefs winners do, you'll be able to tap into the same kind of performance results that winners experience.

Before you develop your visualization power, there are a few how-to procedures you'll need to learn. Whenever you visualize, think of yourself as a projectionist capable of slowing down,

Illustration by John Decker

speeding up, or even freezing a movie. Another critical factor will be to wrap the action with emotion and feeling so that the subconscious can respond to the picture commands as if they were real. There'll be times when you watch yourself perform, and times when you jump into the picture to feel the competitive event as a first person experience with all of its glorious details.

Each time you participate in the imaging process you actually will be improving your game performance. By experiencing the mental workout, you will be dealing directly with the automatic mechanism that controls your volleyball success. No longer will your subconscious have to rely on your old subjective definitions of past play for its input. With the aid of visualization you can store an unlimited amount of winning performances.

Remember your visualization may not be an image at all. It may take the form of a feeling you have or a statement you are saying to yourself. Regardless of its form, clarity, or size, trust us, you've been visualizing. For now, let go of all your doubts and cynicism. Make a sincere effort to keep an open mind. You don't have to fully believe that visualization will work for you, but you will need hope in your heart if you expect to get belief in your head. Has anything great ever been accomplished with a negative attitude? With a little advance trust, proof is on its way.

You can visualize any time or anywhere, but for best results, a deep relaxation procedure is necessary. Once you remember the flow of action you created in the relaxed state, you can visualize while jogging, riding in a bus, waiting in line, sitting in study hall, or watching TV. However, the very best time for mental visualization is while lying in bed before retiring or just before getting out of bed in the morning.

Before your first relaxation and visualization workout we suggest that you either read through the following instructions several times, or record the directions on an audio cassette and listen to your own voice lead you through the visualization exercise. Thousands of athletes have been guided through the visualization process by listening to the audio cassette *Living the Miracle.**

*For information on ordering the cassette, write to ***Living the Miracle* Audio Cassette, Box 134 VB, East Setauket, New York, 11733, or call 516-751-3513.** The cassette is available in nine different sports.

LET YOUR INNER JOURNEY BEGIN

If you're ready, sit back, fully relaxed, in a comfortable chair with both feet uncrossed on the floor. Put your hands on your lap palms up. A deep relaxation response is required so your subconscious can be fully opened to accept the flow of positive impressions it's about to receive. When you finish the mental visualization experience, you will feel both energized and refreshed. If you are about to retire, you can lie on your back in bed, arms and legs fully extended, relaxed, and uncrossed. Afterwards, you'll naturally fall off into a restful sleep. Let your inner journey begin.

The more you relax, let go, and trust in the power of your subconscious, the sooner you'll experience the benefits. Close your eyes and begin to pay attention to your natural breathing rhythm. As you focus on each exhalation, silently say to yourself the command, "Let-go."

Ready,

Let-go: Feel the air escaping through your nose and mouth.

Let-go: You are releasing all tension and doubt.

Let-go: You are becoming more and more relaxed as the air flows outward.

Let-go: Worry and tension are flowing from your body through your fingertips and toes.

Let-go: All concern and doubt are disappearing.

- With each exhalation you are becoming very deeply relaxed.
- All playing limitations and restrictions are permanently pouring out from your body.
- Past mistakes and fears are disappearing forever.
- A safe, trusting feeling fills your body.
- You are now deeply relaxed.
- Every command you hear will create a clear, detailed, positive mental picture.
- The images will be indelibly recorded into the memory bank of your subconscious.
- When needed, they will automatically provide your subconscious with the positive commands of the winner.
- Your reliable power mechanism will accomplish the rest.
  Continue to breathe evenly, but this time focus on the air filling your lungs.
  Each time you inhale feel the sensation of air filling every cell of your body with fresh confidence and energy.

Now,

Inhale: You are unbeatable!

Inhale: You are a winner!

Inhale: You are the best!

Inhale: You are great!

Inhale: You are unstoppable!

- Now, imagine a large funnel at the top of your head.
- As you breathe inwardly, feel a column of bright white energy pouring through the funnel into your head, down your neck, and into your lungs.
- With each inward breath experience a sensation of power flowing through your veins into every muscle, every fiber, every cell, and reaching deep into every atom of your body.
- With each breath feel a sense of radiating self-confidence and strength building up in the center of your body.
- Feel free to draw upon this unlimited energy source anytime you need it during competition. It will always be there to give you the power, trust, and know-how to be all that you want to be in training and in competition.
- You are now deeply relaxed, the ideal state to program your subconscious with positive commands.

To discover your true potential, it's time to decide on a specific playing weakness or attitude, a real problem in your game, one that, if you could magically turn around into a strength, would dramatically improve your game. Is it any of the following?

- A more powerful, accurate spike...perhaps off a quick set
- Precise forearm passing
- A decisive serve for match point
- Quicker feet to set the block and stop the hitter
- More aggressiveness on backcourt defense
- Or simply to play more freely, less uptight

Once you've got a clear-cut purpose for your subconscious to act upon, let's go to the video tape in your mind to direct a new script of images. You are about to discover that to do the impossible, you first must see the invisible.

With your eyes still closed, imagine that the insides of your eyelids have become a large silver video screen. Upon this screen you will visualize the action and moves you want. Each time you imagine yourself vividly serving, passing, setting, hitting, or blocking, your subconscious will receive new positive mental commands that will automatically improve your game. The visualization process, in order to give you optimal effect, will be in three progressive steps.

- Initially you will be only an observer studying the confident movements of a star athlete, someone you admire, who possesses the skill or attitude you desire. Watch the role model perfectly performing, competing, and finishing off the action successfully until you get a clear image of what it takes to perform that specific skill and play at your best.
- In the second step you'll enter the winner's body and go along for the ride. Here it will be a first person slow motion sequence, so you can feel the crucial, dramatic movements of the action. With repeated viewing you'll soon sense a building of confidence — the feeling that you can do it all!
- In the third and final phase of your video success story abandon your role model. Now it's

you playing at game speed in tournament conditions. Visualize the opponent's best playing against you, hear the roar of the hostile or friendly crowd, feel the soft texture of the ball, hear the rubber of your shoes squeaking on the floor, sense your adrenalin pumping. Be sure to feel yourself always completing the action perfectly each time you rerun the video.

Let the mental video tape roll! With your eyes closed, see the champion clearly before you performing decisively — in complete control, smoothly finishing off the perfect play. Now take a few minutes and replay the scene several times until you feel in total control of the movements.

- It's time to jump inside the winner for the slow motion ride. Allow your mind and body to enter the star's body. You and your role model are one! This is a first person, here and now experience. In perfect slow motion, feel the critical, decisive movements as you want them to happen. Once again, clearly, vividly, always succeeding — repeat the slow motion winning sequence several times.

- Now let's go at game speed. Quicken the action, add all the details, sense the excitement and the pressure of the moment. Add a score, a game factor. Is the score tied? Are you down a point? Are you serving? Receiving? What game is it? Second? Last? Whether you're serving, passing, or hitting, be certain to finish off each play perfectly. You are now unstoppable, invincible, at your best, in perfect control. Hear the crowd responding and see your coach, teammates, and friends acknowledging your outstanding performance.

The more often you repeat the video, seeing, hearing, and feeling the sure, confident action, the quicker your body will be conditioned to respond to your mental commands in competition. Replay the video again and again, and you'll understand that it is true, **"You become what you think about!"**

HOW DO YOU FEEL?

Let us ask you:

- In step 1...Were you able to see the star?
- In step 2...Were you able to jump inside the star's body and feel the slow motion winning ride?
- In step 3...Were you able to abandon the winner and feel yourself achieve the successful action?

If the answer is "yes" to all three steps, you're not alone. Most athletes experience little difficulty in seeing and feeling themselves getting it done. Although science cannot explain how we're capable of doing it, they know for certain that each time someone experiences an imagined event, the central nervous system accepts the unreal experience as real, especially if the imagined experience is wrapped with a sense of feeling.

AN OLYMPIAN VISUALIZES

So now you know where the power switch for your inner success system is located. In your mind's eye! Winners have long used this power to help themselves get what they want. Don't you think it's time that you do the same? Listen to what Mike Powell, the world record holder in the broad jump, said about the power of visualization and his famous jump:

"When I was a kid, I would run down the hallway of my house, plant my lead foot just outside of the kitchen, and jump through the dining room, into the den, over the green shag carpeting, and I would land somewhere in front of my mom's red leather easy chair. It was on these occasions, as I danced around the room imagining that I had just broken the world record, that my mom would usually point out that I had scratched on my take off, or that my jump was wind-aided. My mom was a real comedian.

But then one day, I'm 27 years old and I'm in Tokyo, and the scoreboard tells me I'm in second place. So I take off down the runway, hit the board clean, and leave the ground. And I think about reindeer, and dunking from the free-throw line, and gliders, and slingshots, and Sir Isaac Newton, and air. And then everything gets really quiet. And as I stare at the horizon, at the peak of my jump, I think I see, just for a second, my mom's red leather easy chair at the end of the pit."

AN ATHLETE LIVES HER DREAM

Steve Dallman, formerly the head coach at the University of Southern Mississippi, had previously worked as the head of the National Volleyball Institute in Manteno, Illinois. During his time there, he had the opportunity to meet a young lady by the name of Mary De Carlo. Mary came to Steve in June of 1991 and asked if he would help train her to become a better setter. She was going to be a senior and knowing her previous season had been spent on the bench, Steve realized there was much work to be done on all aspects of her game.

Steve told Mary he would help her if she would agree to three training rules:

1. Put in eight hours of training on the court each week.
2. Learn to believe in herself.
3. Trust everything Steve told her.

Steve wasted no time in testing Mary's commitment to become a starter. He recommended she listen to Stan's audio action cassette *Living the Miracle* each and every day. Mary committed to Steve's inner and outer game training program, working exceptionally hard throughout the summer. There were times Mary became discouraged and considered quitting, but because of Steve's constant encouragement she didn't. When the high school volleyball season ended, Steve was not surprised that his dedicated student had won the starting setter position, and had been named to the All-Area Team. Playing in the area All-Star game, Mary De Carlo had also won the most coveted Special Determination Award. Not too shabby for a girl who didn't get much playing time as a junior!

Are you ready to pay the same price Mary did so that you can live your dream?

WINNERS SEE WHAT THEY WANT

Bill Walton, the head coach at the University of Houston, employed a unique visualization technique to aid his team in pulling off a major upset during the 1996 Conference USA semi-finals in Louisville. Bill's Cougars were facing Louisville's own nationally ranked Cardinals, a team they had lost to twice during the regular season. Playing nearly perfect volleyball, Houston won the first game but then faltered in game two, losing 6-15.

Because the game was being televised on ESPN, there was a ten minute intermission before game three. After reviewing their strategy Bill gathered his players together, but instead of ending the session with the traditional "Cougar Cheer," he did something very unusual. He asked his players and coaches to join in a circle, grasping hands above their heads, and in a low whisper he said, "I have a question for everybody in this huddle. Can everybody see themselves celebrating a victory after the match?" A few seconds passed and he repeated, "Can you see the celebration?" After a long pause the group answered in one emotional voice, "Yes!" Then their coach said, "Well let's go get it!"

Experiencing the excitement of the moment, Bill Walton's assistant coach approached him on the way to the court and exclaimed, "I'm so pumped I've got goosebumps. You've got me so excited I'm ready to play." And play the Cougars did. They surprised their opponents by taking two hard fought games to win the match 3-2. If you're looking for the moral of the story, maybe it's this: **Winners see what they want!**

ANOTHER COACH DISCOVERS VOLLEYBALL CYBERNETICS

During the summer of 1989, Pam Kurtz took her Birch Run High School team to the **"Yes, I Can!" Camp** in Saginaw, Michigan. The previous season Pam's team struggled with a 4-32 record. To say the least, she was desperate.

With nothing to lose and everything to gain, Pam decided to make the visualization and affirmation exercises she learned at camp a part of her program. During the rest of that summer, through club ball and into the high school season, the Birch Run players used Stan's audio action tape on a daily basis. The result? Pam's team did a 180 degree turnaround! Birch Run compiled a dramatic 44-7 record and a District Championship as well.

The Birch Run success story did not end there. Pam recalls the unforgettable season of 1992: "Beyond a lack of size, without a single player taller than 5'8", we were considered as having the least athletic team in our league. But the girls kept working and believing in themselves and each other. In practice and matches, we were using goal cards and employing a lot of the other inner game methods learned at camp."

Pam's team was also winning games. A final record of 53-11, winners of seven of eight tournaments, a District Title, a Regional Title, and a trip to the Final Four of the Michigan Class B State Finals all confirmed that this was a very special team on a very special mission! Not bad for a so-called "unathletic" group of girls with the biggest player only 5'8".

As Pam's team traveled through their incredible season, they were often asked how the team kept on winning. Their simple answer: "We mentally practice being winners."

Inch By Inch, It's A Cinch

Maxwell Maltz writes in his classic book, *Psycho-Cybernetics,* **"Once you give your subconscious a definite goal to achieve, you can depend upon your automatic mechanism to take you to that goal. But to accomplish this, you must think of the end result in terms of a present possibility. If you keep your positive goal in mind and picture it to yourself so vividly as to make it real and think of it in terms of an accomplished fact, you will experience the self-confidence, courage, and faith you will need to achieve the goal."**

Together, let's prove Maltz's concept is right. But rather than go for the whole ball of wax at one time and turn a specific skill from **"a chump to a champ"** level, let's do it gradually. An inch or two at a time will be easier to achieve. There will be less chance for jamming your success mechanism with overtrying.

Weightlifters start with gradual increments and so can you. Determine a goal which you can attain without overtrying. We're only asking you to lower your sights so that you can ease into the habit of success. If you agree, follow these steps:

1. Review the inventory you took in the chapter on Self-Awareness. In the first step of the **FAST** formula on goal setting, we asked you to pick two offensive, defensive, and attitude skills you wanted to improve. Now numerically establish an increased score of two as your new performance goal.

2. Close your eyes and think about the particular score you gave yourself on a specific skill and raise it by two. Hold that number in your mind until you can answer this question: What would you have to do on the court to earn that higher score? How well would you have to play? If it's a #7 level of performance you want, help yourself by identifying someone who consistently plays on that higher level. Think of how he or she performs to rate the higher score. Once you can conceptualize what you're looking for, your subconscious will know exactly what it has to do.

3. For example, imagine that you're observing a player performing a #7 serving skill you want. Is it a confident, aggressive serve? Keep visualizing until you're ready to jump into the picture and make it your own first person, winning experience. Imagine competing with the same speed, force, and finish as your #7 role model. Repeat the inside-out visualization a dozen times until you feel you have it.

4. Regarding this skill, evaluate your performance at the end of each practice or match. Don't be concerned that it's subjective. As soon as you achieve the higher score, then challenge yourself with an even higher score. Go for that #8.

You have a list of skills and attitudes you can work on. Go to it. Inch by inch...it'll be a cinch!

A COACH WANTS MORE

In the fall of 1985, Sue Subich was coaching at Ashland Crestview High School. This is her Volleyball Cybernetics success story.

"The previous year we had reached the Regional semi-finals. After leading the third game 12-5, we lost to Mogadore High. As you can imagine our team was very disappointed. Knowing that I had many of the players returning the following season, I forced them to go back to the gym and watch the regional final between Mogadore and Black River. Black River was in our league and we had beaten them twice in the regular season. Black River won the match and earned a trip to the State Tournament (Final Four). My kids were feeling really down knowing that Black River was going to State and they were going home.

Over the following summer, I worked the **"Yes, I Can!" Volleyball Camp.** There were many innovative concepts that I decided to use with my team the next season. One of the tools I took back from camp was an audio tape entitled, **Living the Miracle.** I made this tape available to each of my players and told them about the power of visualization. Several of my better athletes decided to give the tape a chance. They played it every night before they went to bed, visualizing themselves and our team performing perfectly play after play. Interestingly, many of these players who were getting results never admitted to their teammates that they continually used the tape until after the season.

Also before every match I took my entire team through a series of relaxation and visualization exercises. In competition they seemed more focused and ready to play. Even during time-outs we made it a team habit to have each girl close her eyes, concentrate on her breathing rhythm and then visualize a successful performance.

It all worked! The season was a dream. We completed the regular season 22-0 and were ranked #1 in Ohio. We then proceeded to march all the way through postseason play to the State Tournament. It was an incredibly exciting time for our school and the entire community. We won the semi-finals before losing to the perennial power, St. Henry, in the final. What I liked about our team is that we learned to play without fear of failure. Much of our success I credit to Stan Kellner and his **"Yes, I Can!"** concepts.

Just a side note on Pam Conley, a senior on that team. She was named first team All-Ohio. A powerful hitter and a solid defensive player, Pam told me months after our season was over how much the **"Yes, I Can!"** tape helped her achieve her best season. She admitted that before starting to use the audio tape, she had always become physically ill from nervousness before every match. The relaxation series helped her attain a power state by redirecting her adrenaline in a positive manner. She was able to concentrate on what she wanted to accomplish instead of what she wanted to avoid."

Two Time State Coach of the Year Sue Subich has taken her **Yes, You Can!** coaching attitude to the Division I power Mansfield Madison. Her team's accomplishments: Regional qualifier ('88, '91-'96), State qualifier ('93), State Poll Champs ('94-'95) and State Tournament Champs ('97).

A Spectacular Recovery

For years, many in the medical profession have been proclaiming the benefits of mental visualization in the healing of injuries. Dave's partner at the Ohio **"Yes, I Can!" Volleyball Camp,** Joe Kolodka experienced this amazing power first hand, or "first heal" as it turned out. A few years ago Joe suffered a horrible injury while playing in an adult volleyball league match. He had severely torn his Achilles tendon. His doctor told him he had torn 80% of his Achilles. They told him because of his age (39) it would be at least a year before he would be able to do any kind of even light physical activity, let alone play volleyball.

Knowing the powers of visualization, Joe decided to do what he could to speed up his lengthy recovery process. Every night as he lay in bed just before falling asleep, Joe would visualize the fibers of his Achilles tendon healing back together. Did it help? Nine months after the injury happened, Joe was jogging! The rest of his dramatic recovery was far ahead of schedule as well. His physical therapist was simply amazed! To this day Joe firmly believes that "seeing" the tendon fibers heal was responsible for his spectacular recovery.

So the next time you experience an injury, after you get the proper medical advice and start your treatment, start visualizing the recovery.

A Review: How To Use Visualization To Improve Your Game

1. Decide what you want to achieve. This can be the mastery of a skill, the solving of a problem, or the development of a positive habit or attitude. Make this your goal. Winning starts at the beginning. Set specific goals.

2. Decide why you want to achieve your goal. You must have a reason that is important to yourself. You'll need to have a strong purpose in order to commit to the daily visualization exercises of **Volleyball Cybernetics.**

3. Write your goal down on a goal card (see pg. 36). Put the goal card in your bedroom where you will always see it before you retire at night. This could be next to your alarm clock, on your night stand, or on the mirror of your dresser. Make copies of it and place them where you will see them at various times throughout your day. This could be on the inside door of your school locker or inside the cover of a folder you normally carry around. This will help you to stay focused on your goal, as well as be a reminder to do the visualization exercises each night before falling asleep.

4. Find someone who has already mastered your goal. Watch him or her perform and learn to develop your own mental video of this performance. This can be done either by watching your role model live or on videotape. Once you have developed a strong mental picture of your role model performing, replace him or her in the video with yourself. Keep watching your new mental video until you have a strong memory of it.

5. Each night when you go to bed, play side one of the *Living the Miracle* audio cassette. This will help you achieve the relaxed state necessary for the visualization exercises.

6. The more often you do the visualization exercises, the better.

Chapter Seven

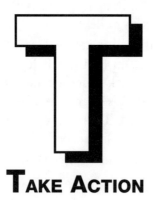

TAKE ACTION

"Do or do not, there is no try."
Yoda

In order to live your volleyball dream, you will need to take persistent and decisive action. Your vision of success will remain nothing more than a series of hopes, wishes, and fanciful thoughts unless action is on your daily menu. This means finding the courage to do the thing that is hard to do in training and matches. The opposite of taking action is avoidance, and you already know that road leads nowhere near where winners travel.

If action is so essential, why don't we all take action? What state of mind separates the winners from the losers — the achievers from the underachievers? The answer lies in the underachievers' fear of consequences. Losers are afraid of the feeling that is associated with failing. Their fear of pain, embarrassment, guilt, and feelings of unworthiness force them to ride in the slow lane of life. They tend to search out reasons why they shouldn't take action. Winners, on the other hand, never think about messing up. They are motivated with reasons that allow them to pay any price necessary to take decisive and persistent action.

The next time you're faced with taking action or playing it safe ask yourself:

"What will I lose if I don't take action?"

Then see if you're not driven **to do the thing that is hard to do.** Losers usually ask the mother of all disempowering questions, **What will I lose if I take action and fail?**

THE CRYSTAL BALL METHOD

A method used at the **"Yes, I Can!" Volleyball Camp** to encourage athletes to find training commitment is called **The Crystal Ball Method.** Have some fun with our **Crystal Ball Method** and see if you don't suddenly find the commitment to work on your weak skills in practice and matches. Follow these steps:

Think about a weak skill holding you back from becoming the player you want to be. Something you should have been working on in competition long ago. Sit back in a comfortable chair. Relax and close your eyes.

Imagine a big, misty crystal ball in front of you, one with magical powers of seeing into the future. Look into it. See the mist within the ball clearing. In the crystal ball you see yourself performing that weak skill in an important match against your arch rival. How are you doing? Are you messing it up? Of course you are! That's why it's a weakness. Look closely into the crystal ball and tell us what your teammates, coach, and friends are saying about you behind your back. Can you see your own image? How do you look and feel? Is that a happy, confident face staring back at you?

Now still holding the crystal ball, it's time to travel two years into the future. Because you never took the time or expended the energy to turn that weak skill around, you're still saddled with it. Look into the crystal ball. What is it you see? What are your teammates and coach saying about your game? How many opportunities have been lost because of this terrible weakness? Now that another season has passed with too many unfulfilled games, how do you appear in that crystal ball? Are you playing strong and courageous, or can you see pain and frustration in your face? Not a pretty scene is it?

Let's project much farther into the future. Your playing days are over, and you're looking back upon your playing career. What do you see in the crystal ball? Are you seeing yourself fulfilled, happy, and satisfied? As a result of never improving that weak skill, what do you see? Is it an unhappy, depressed, and unfulfilled image looking back at you?

Consider what would happen if you decided to commit to turning that weakness around? Let's say you committed to everything recommended in this book, plus you worked hard in practice and played that flaw in matches until it gradually became an incredible asset. Look into the crystal ball and tell us what you see.

It's the next season. Imagine a volleyball coming your way in a decisive match winning situation. You're playing a strong skill that once was that extraordinary weakness. Confidence abounds! What do you see yourself doing in the game? Is it successful? Yes, it is! Now what are your teammates, coach, and friends saying about your performance? See your own reflection in the crystal ball. Are you wearing a pleased and proud expression on your face? You bet you are!

Project two years into the future. Think about all the matches you contributed in because you developed that ready for prime time skill. How do your parents and teammates feel about your ability to step-up and perform in the clutch? Find yourself in that crystal ball and tell us what you see. Notice the confidence and inner strength that your image is exuding.

Let's take the final step far into the future. Your playing career is over. Look back at your accomplishments in the crystal ball. Think about all the matches you were able to impact because you were willing to work on that playing weakness and turn it into a strength.

There you have the **Crystal Ball Method.** You've taken both a painful and joyful ride into the future. Which one did you prefer? Now that you are back to the present, what are your plans? Do you feel compelled to take immediate action? Time flies! Feel the courage to take action. You are no longer locked into the past. Nothing is holding you back. So take action...now!

WHAT WOULD YOU ATTEMPT TO DO IF YOU COULDN'T FAIL?

What a great concept! Think about the creative and aggressive action you would take in your next match if you couldn't fail. Which serve would you attempt? What chances would you be willing to take on defense, if you couldn't fail? The fact is you can't fail if you really think about it! The worst scenario is you end up with a valuable "learning experience." Consider that the next time you walk on the court.

When challenged by those wonderful "learning experiences," think, "What's the worst thing that can happen to me?" This is a question Stan often asks himself when faced with a "should I" or "shouldn't I" situation. Let Stan tell you in his own words how he found unexpected courage to take sudden action.

Several years ago, after finishing a camp in Colorado, my wife and I decided to experience white water rafting. There were twelve of us in a large gray rubber raft enjoying the adventure of our lives. As we glided down the Colorado River anticipating the white water rapids that lay ahead, little did I realize that this adventure would be even more exciting than expected. I was located in the front of the raft with a paddle in my hands. My main responsibility was to keep us in the middle of the river.

A hundred yards ahead of us in the white water, I noticed nine small individually operated kayaks skillfully being maneuvered in various patterns and formations. As they came out of a figure eight formation, the kayakers joined hands and formed a single circle. With the front of the kayaks facing inside (tails out), the circle of kayaks gracefully slid over the churning white water.

What happened next was truly amazing. One of the paddlers sprung out of his kayak and proceeded to jump from the rear of one kayak to another, around the circle of kayaks until he safely returned to his own kayak. This dangerous action was followed by a second man who emerged from his kayak juggling three tennis balls in his hands. Without dropping a ball, he completed his dance around the outer edge of the circle of kayaks! I couldn't believe what I was witnessing! Then a third kayaker, a courageous woman, successfully took her turn. This was all happening while the unit of kayaks in this star formation rode the unpredictable rapids.

I remember thinking, "What a thrill they must be having," when suddenly, our raft collided with the circle of kayaks. Before I could think about what I was doing, I found myself stepping out of my raft and leaping onto the circle of kayaks. Incredibly, I was prancing from one kayak to another! My wife couldn't believe it. Our guide couldn't believe it. The kayakers couldn't believe it. And I certainly couldn't believe what I was doing. I had made no conscious decision to take action. I just did it. As our raft converged with the kayaks, I remember realizing this was a rare opportunity to have some fun, and if I didn't take action, it would quickly pass. Taking action to complete that jaunt around the circle of kayaks will always remain one of my greatest memories.

FINDING THE HIDDEN POWER TO TAKE ACTION

Here are some additional steps for learning how to take action:

- **Set specific, daily goals and achieve them.** Determine short range goals that challenge you. They must be specific and reachable. Your subconscious responds best with clear-cut specific requests. Is it a daily challenge of a total of 100 pushups, 100 situps, or 50 top spin serves to serving zone 5? Whatever short range goals you set, stay with each one of them until finished.
- **Use the power of your imagination.** Develop a feeling of certainty that success is inevitable by vividly imagining the successful outcome in advance. See it, think it, feel it, and let nothing stop you from doing it!
- **Anchor* for power.** There is no better or quicker way to tap your inner resources for prime time action and risk taking than anchoring into a powerful state of mind. Make it a habit to anchor your great moments of strength, courage, and confidence whenever you are on a roll. Employ a key word like **Great!** and some hand action such as slapping your hands together while you're in an intense state of confidence. The power state is now deposited for future use. The key to opening your emotional vault is the sound and touch of your anchor. Then, should you need an emotional pick-up to take action, rapidly fire off several success anchors. Will it work? Stan has lost count of the number of times he has used his energy anchor during the long summer of camps.

* Anchoring is explained in detail in the next chapter.

"CARPE DIEM!"

If all else fails, just do it! Feel the pain, the fear, the unworthiness, the guilt and take action anyway. **Life is short** is a reality factor you cannot ignore. Before you know it, your volleyball playing opportunities will pass as they have for the great ones and the not so great ones. Time does not stand still or wait, but it does run out for all of us. You can't put time into rewind and relive what you've lost. Don't you have a responsibility to yourself to live each day to the fullest?

A coaching friend gave Stan an unforgettable quotation, **"Today I gave the best I had. For what I've kept I've lost forever!"** Don't let a day go by without taking some action to improve your game. Give each moment everything you have and you'll never have to say the saddest of all words, "I coulda...woulda...shoulda!"

A MOVIE MAKES A POINT

Did you see the movie *Dead Poets Society?* There is an unforgettable scene where Robin Williams's character, an odd ball English professor at a boys' prep school in New England, is teaching the concept of fully living each moment of life. To dramatize the lesson, he takes his students into the lobby outside his classroom where trophies and photographs of past championship teams are gathering dust in the trophy case. "I want you to look carefully at those photographs, boys. Perhaps you may have taken them for granted." He continues, "Some of these teams competed over a hundred years ago. Get closer and study the faces of these athletes. Notice they look just like you, boys. Do you know where these athletes are now? They are fertilizer for dandelions!"

Cupping one hand to his ear, he continues, "Can you hear their voices? Listen to what they are telling you. Hear their legacy before it's too late and you become a forgotten photograph lost in a trophy case." He pauses and then whispers in a ghostly voice, **"Carpe...Carpe...Carpe Diem...seize the day, boys! That is what their ghosts are telling you to do! Listen to them begging you to seize each moment you have and live an extraordinary life!"**

Are you ready to seize the moment and live an extraordinary life before your playing days are over? Living life to the fullest is your ultimate challenge! Take action, now, before it's too late, good friend.

This completes the four basic steps of the FAST formula:

F... find a goal and a reason for wanting it.

A... act as if you have the same beliefs, body language, and self-talk of the winner.

S... see yourself succeeding.

T... take action until you achieve what you want.

To win the inner battle and become the player you desire to be, you'll need to know how to eliminate life's greatest waste of energy... frustration. Next up... the Cybernetic how-to.

PART THREE

The Battle Within...

"Never, Never, Never Quit."
Winston Churchill

Chapter Eight

HOW TO ELIMINATE FRUSTRATION

"Those whom the gods wish to destroy they first make mad."
Longfellow

If human potential is pure energy, one of the greatest wastes of energy has to be frustration. What if you could instantly erase the emotional debris of a past mistake by simply pushing a control key on the keyboard of your mental computer? Think of it, you'd be free to compete with the same emotionally clear head of the winner.

Well, there is a mental key you can push that is similar to the button on an electronic word processor. It's called **CLEAR!** Of course, you'll need to program the **CLEAR!** response into your mental computer, but that won't take too long. Are you up to spending a few minutes a day anchoring the word **CLEAR!** until it sticks? Commit to **CLEAR!** and you won't be struggling with the negative energy of frustration anymore… unless you want to.

HOW TO PROGRAM "CLEAR!"

1. Focus your eyes on any plain, white, uncluttered, clear surface such as a section of a white wall or ceiling or the back of a white T-shirt and memorize what you see.
2. As you concentrate on the surface, say the word **CLEAR!** either aloud or to yourself.
3. Next, close your eyes and imagine the same clear, white surface on the inside of your eyelids. As you do, again recite the word **CLEAR!** either aloud or to yourself.
4. Alternate opening and closing your eyelids for one minute. As you focus on the white surface with your eyelids open, recite the word **CLEAR!** and then repeat **CLEAR!** as you imagine the same clear, white surface on the inside of your closed eyelids.

Once you can mentally visualize the white surface with your eyes closed, let's test the anchoring or linking process. Close your eyes and recall a recent poor serve or defensive mistake you made in your last match or practice. Can you recapture the frustration of the moment? With your eyes still closed, say the word **CLEAR!** What happened? Were you able to imagine a clear surface? Did the emotional response of the mistake disappear? If it did, congratulations! The anchoring process was effectively programmed. If you were not able to picture the clear surface on the first try, you are not alone. Only about twenty percent of our campers clear on the initial attempt. Return to the four-step programming procedure until you successfully **Clear!** after an imagined mistake.

TESTING "CLEAR!" ON THE COURT

The next time you make a mistake, calmly recite the anchor word **CLEAR!** Repeat the anchor on every error you make until you achieve a clearing of your mind. Continue to sharpen your clearing ability away from the court, also, for a few minutes a day and you'll appreciate the payoff.

MORE HELP FOR ELIMINATING FRUSTRATION

If you don't like the meaning of something, change it! When things don't go your way, you don't have to feel frustrated, unless you want to. **Framing** can help you respond in a positive way when you don't like the meaning of what just happened to you on the court. By putting a **new frame** around the bad experience, you can change the negative effect of the event. The two types of **framing** are **preframing** and **reframing.**

Coach Mike Gibson employs both **preframing** and **reframing** with his team at the University of Michigan at Dearborn. **"Preframing,"** the Coach explains, "is the act of putting the frame around a situation in advance. You are telling someone how to feel before anything happens. Hollywood calls this the **preview of coming attractions.** Statements like 'You're gong to love this,' 'Wait till you see this,' 'This is going to be so much fun,' etc. set up the listener to expect to feel good in advance of a particular event. For example, I tell my team during practice, 'I've got a new drill that is so great today,' or 'When you pass the ball to the target, everything is going to start to click and we are going to have a great game!' Telling your team in advance 'how to feel' increases their opportunities for success."

The innovative coach describes the **reframing** technique this way, **"Reframing** is changing the meaning of words, phrases or even events so that my players react in a positive way. For example, the team always reframes the word **problem** into the word **challenge.** By doing this, every time we consider the word **problem** we instantly change it to **challenge.** For most people the word **problem** has a negative meaning — something they have to deal with. We believe that the word **challenge** gets our players excited about finding the solution. After a while, **problems** automatically become **challenges** and they are much easier and more fun to solve."

THE ART OF REFRAMING WITH THE HELP OF VISUALIZATION

Everybody makes mistakes. Volleyball is a game of mistakes. But have you noticed that some athletes keep making the same mistakes over and over again? Then there are others who make a mistake, learn from it, and move on. Which group do you belong to? Learn the art of reframing and your mistakes won't become a series of self-fulfilling prophecies for making more mistakes.

Reframing in a sense is the art of turning frustration into fascination by changing a mistake or an unfavorable experience into a productive learning experience. By improving the way you look at the experience, you can turn any negative event into an advantage. The winner believes, "There are no mistakes, only learning experiences."

Begin the reframing process by asking yourself what you have learned from the negative experience. Your answer will help you avoid the mistake in the future. Your imagination will guide your **Reticular Activating System** into helping your subconscious to produce a better performance. Learn how to follow bothersome playing habits with a smart question like, "What have I learned?"

Reframe new meaning to a stubborn mistake by going to a quiet place, away from the action and...

1. Close your eyes, relax, and imagine yourself making a playing mistake.
2. Ask yourself what skill or attitude you must develop so this mistake doesn't happen again.
3. Identify someone you know who performs this skill with ease.
4. Imagine the role model performing the skill in competition (outside-in view).
5. Jump inside the mental movie and in slow motion feel yourself inside the star performing the successful action (inside-out).
6. Now abandon the star. Feel yourself performing the skill in the match at competitive speed, finishing off the play perfectly (inside-out).
7. Feel how good it feels to have performed the skill successfully!

Winners instinctively reframe. You must too. Reframing your mistakes into learning experiences will help you to become the prime time player of your dreams.

DAVE REFRAMES A NEGATIVE INTO A POSITIVE

Both winning athletes and coaches have the habit of instinctively looking for good when "the going gets tough." They understand the importance of reframing negatives into golden opportunities. During the second half of the '94 season, Dave used a reframing technique to turn around a potentially troublesome situation and help his team face a huge challenge in a key match. His team was tied for first in the conference with only a few matches left. The next match would be the key to achieving their goal of repeating as conference champions. Unfortunately they had to travel to Elyria West to play in a gym where Dave's Wildcats had experienced victory only once before in the school's entire history. At the time West was playing their best volleyball of the season and only trailed Dave's team by a game in the league standings.

As his Wildcats took the court for warm-ups, Dave couldn't help but notice something was dramatically different in the gym. Over in the corner of the bleachers on the Wildcats' side was something neither Dave nor his girls had ever seen before at any of their matches. For the first time ever a loud Elyria West Pep Band was cranking up the volume. The wily coach of the Wolverines had decided to pull out all the stops in an effort to psyche out Dave's Wildcats. The atmosphere in the gym became even more intense as the pep band played as loudly as they could. Dave could see that his players seemed stunned as they were unable to even talk to one another. Trouble was brewing in his girls' eyes. Quickly Dave sprang into action. **"Hey, this is great!"** he preframed as he moved among his players with a big smile on his face. **"This is fun! They don't think they're good enough to beat us! That's why they need the band. The psyche job won't work because they know they can't beat us!"**

As Dave continued to show his enthusiasm for the thundering music, he could see his players start to smile as they were catching his optimistic attitude. Their faces continued smiling as the Wildcats went into hitting lines. The entire team was suddenly moving on the court with complete confidence. They knew that their coach was right. West was trying to psyche them out with a gimmick. All of a sudden, it had become fun warming up to the jamming pep band.

When the match started the Wildcats came out on fire. They crushed their opponents in two hard fought games. Dave's girls had taken the presence of the pep band that was there to put pressure on them, and reframed it to their advantage. Thanks to some strategic reframing by their coach, the Wildcats' victory that evening was the last major battle on the way to the school's second consecutive conference championship.

What Dave's team accomplished, you can too. The next time you're faced with a negative situation that is upsetting, turn it into a positive by asking yourself, **"What's good about it?"** Then start reframing before it's too late, and your negative mindset leads you to failure!

THE ERASURE TECHNIQUE

There'll be times when a stubborn skill, weakness, or attitude cannot be easily reprogrammed. Although you faithfully follow each step of the reframing process, the losing skill or attitude refuses to disappear. Learn the Erasure Technique.

- Pretend that you are watching memories of some of your most embarrassing serves. For example, one of your playing habits is serving into the net, especially on key serves. Imagine in this movie seeing yourself drive one serve after another into the net. Mentally see yourself misdirect a series of serves into the net for several minutes.

- Now start at the end of one of those bad memories and run the movie backwards at triple the speed. In other words, see everything going in reverse. The ball is coming off the net backwards and is returning to your hand. While you see everything happening in reverse, simultaneously hear amusing sounds like a nickelodeon or circus music playing in the background. Can you see all the action in your favorite color?
- Now, run the movie forward at super speed and imagine that Mickey Mouse ears are growing out of the heads of the other players. Imagine the noses of all the players are getting longer and turning pink. Hear the happy music and keep running this memory of the serve going into the net, backwards and forwards, faster and faster, until every time you just think about serving into the net, you smile or laugh.

See what you've done? By employing the **Erasure Technique,** you've scratched the painful mental tape you have on serving into the net and permanently damaged it to the point that it can't be played anymore without you smiling. Enjoy your new freedom.

TEAM REFRAMING: THE CIRCLE OF "WHOOSH!"

Are you ready for the mother of all weird programming techniques **"Whoosh!"**? Walk into a **"Yes, I Can!" Camp** at the end of any game, and you will observe both teams circled up vigorously applauding their mistakes! No, they haven't lost their minds, they're regaining control by reframing as a unit. This is our Cybernetic step-by-step **Team Whooshing** procedure:

1. The team circles up. Each player thinks about one frustrating mistake he or she made during a match and starts applauding. All applaud at the same time.
2. On the command of "ready," they stop clapping, make two fists and then open their hands toward the floor as if they were purging the emotions of the mistake from their bodies. As they do this, they all shout the word **Whoosh!**
3. After the **Whoosh!** they take a quiet moment and reframe the mistake. They imagine seeing themselves successfully executing the skill they had performed poorly in the game. First outside-in. Then inside out (first person experience) at game speed.
4. They finish by applauding their imagined success as a team.

If you're a coach, we know the method sounds wacky. **Team Whooshing** offers players a great opportunity for a quick state change as well as a synergistic opportunity to visualize together. After scrimmaging, try **Team Whooshing** for a week and you may just notice your players competing with an increased level of freedom and togetherness.

For the athlete, we recommend you individually **Whoosh** at home. Think about a mistake, applaud it, **Whoosh** it, and reframe. Just make sure the door is tightly closed behind you.

THE "SWISH!" METHOD

No, it's not the sound of the ball flying by your ear on a kill. **Swish!** is an inner game method for eliminating your most persistent playing problems. Originally the **Swish Pattern** was developed by Richard Bandler as a key **NLP (Neuro-Linguistic Programming) Technique** for overcoming negative habits such as procrastination. The first time Stan introduced **Swish!** was to a player at camp who was experiencing a problem common to many players, a loss of confidence as soon as her high school coach back home started yelling at her. She was having trouble maintaining her composure any time her coach screamed instructions. The coach's disappointed facial expression and angry tone of voice unhinged her. The player's concern was, "I feel that I have to play perfectly to stay in the match." Since her soft self-image was doing the talking, her faithful subconscious was doing the overtrying.

The player was putting needless pressure on herself. Instead of competing aggressively, her play was tentative and tight. The wrong kind of thinking was making her life miserable and her game inconsistent.

This is what Stan asked the athlete to do:

"Can you remember the last time you felt frustrated after the coach responded in a way that upset you? Close your eyes and relive that scene. Make that mental image big and bright and see it directly in front of you, in your mind's eye, until you can recapture exactly how bad you felt.

- With your eyes still closed, I want you to imagine placing the picture (tightening up in competition) into the palm of your left hand. That's right, mentally put it as an image into the palm of your left hand. Imagine it staying there.

- Now with your eyes still closed, I want you to create a movie of the person you'd really like to be under pressure. The ideal you. The player you truly want to become. Can you remember a time, or even just imagine a time, when you were brimming with confidence, when you did everything right on the court? Nothing could bother you. You were strong, unstoppable, and decisive. I don't care how brief the moment or who you were playing against, just recall the powerful state of mind you were enjoying at that precise moment.

- Make that picture even bigger and more vivid than the first one; then I want you to imagine it shrinking and becoming a tight, compact, small ball of energy. Place it into the palm of your right hand. Squeeze that hand into a clenched fist and feel the imaginary ball of positive energy within your fist. It's the ideal person you want to be rolled into a tight ball in the fist of your right hand.

- Next, with your eyes still closed, yell the word **Swish!** as you punch the fist of your right hand that is holding the image of the **ideal you** into the palm of your left hand that is holding the image of the **old you.** At the moment of contact feel the new picture shatter the old mental picture into a thousand small pieces. All that is left now is the big, bright picture of the **new you.**

Repeat the **Swish!** pattern a half dozen times in rapid succession. Get excited and shout **Swish!** each time you punch your fist into the palm. Feel the new image bursting through the old image, destroying it into tiny bits and pieces and then replacing it. Don't stop! Keep doing it again and again. Repetition and speed are important. Feel the breakthrough. Envision the image of the ideal you in your mind's eye. Feel the triumph and the victory.

Now it's time to see if your reconditioned thinking has collapsed the old negative anchor you've associated with your coach's behavior. Let's see if **Swish!** has really created the confident state you want.

Think about your coach reacting strongly to a mistake you made in a recent match. Feel the frustration and fear as you think about your coach yelling at you.

Say **Swish!** to yourself, simultaneously driving the fist of your right hand into the open palm of your left hand. (If you're a lefty, let your dominant hand be the fist.)

Now, repeat the action several times until you feel your state of mind change."

Stan asked, "How do you feel?" With a big grin across her face, she said, "I feel tremendous... fantastic! The second I thought about my coach, I felt a surge of power in my body."

"The real test would be in your next match," Stan explained, "but until then, keep reinforcing the **Swish!** anchor whenever you experience a tightening feeling for whatever reason. Be as inconspicuous as you can when you drive your fist into your palm. Remember to think **Swish** as you do."

YOUR BOWL OF LIGHT

Whenever Stan is in Hawaii he takes the opportunity to talk to the young men incarcerated at the Koolau Youth Correctional Facility situated on the windward side of the Island of Oahu. The visit to the facility is as painful as it is rewarding. In stark contrast to the island paradise with its majestic mountains, dancing blue waters, and proud and joyous Hawaiian people, the jail is filled to capacity with defeated teenagers gone astray because of the wrong kind of thinking and doing.

Stan was saddened to discover over 80 percent of them will repeat their incarceration. Why is this so? In spite of the pain of imprisonment attached to their past behavior, they are still not ready to change their strategy of living, nor change the disempowering beliefs responsible for getting them there. A teacher at the facility told Stan that one of their faults is that they never learned how to develop problem solving skills. They can't handle their emotions when things go wrong.

On one of Stan's trips to Hawaii, he met Umar Rahsaan. Umar is a fifth grade teacher at a small elementary school on the other side of the island, away from the jail. While visiting his classroom, Stan was instantly filled with fascination and excitement. The colorful mural covered walls of the classroom were in complete contrast to the depressing gray surroundings of the jail. The vivid, pastel illustrations were entirely created by his gifted students and produced a feeling of adventure, purpose, and discovery. Throughout the room there were projects depicting the history of the people of the world at work and play. As Stan stepped into this sanctuary of learning, he felt he was in a special place of love and appreciation.

It was there in that room Stan found an ancient Hawaiian saying scripted on a plain piece of brown paper centrally placed on an old wooden table for everyone to see. The table sat next to a window overlooking a mountain very similar to the mountain that borders the correctional facility. Rich with optimism, the saying's simple advice expressed a message of hope that Stan only wished could be memorized as a code of behavior by the young inmates at the Correctional Facility at Koolau.

The next time you get overwhelmed with frustration, anger, and disappointment, read this untitled Hawaiian saying:

"Each child born has, at birth, a bowl of perfect light. If he tends to his light, it will grow in strength and he can do all things. Swim with the sharks, fly with the birds, know and understand all things. If, however, he becomes envious, jealous, angry, frustrated, negative or fearful, he drops a stone into his bowl of light and some of the light goes out. Light and the stone cannot hold the same space. If he continues to put stones in the bowl of light, the light will go out and he will become a stone himself. A stone does not grow, nor does it move. If at any time, he tires of being a stone, all he needs to do is turn the bowl upside down and the stones will fall away and the light will grow once more." (Ancient Hawaiian Saying)

The very next time Stan returned to Koolau, he brought a large wooden bowl and some lava rocks of different sizes. He asked the young men to think about whom they hated. Stan asked one of them to pick the size of a rock that closely represented his feelings regarding this person. "Now drop the rock into the bowl," he said. After a half dozen rocks were placed in the bowl representing various negative emotions, Stan passed the heavy bowl around the room for all of them to hold. Then he said to the last one who held the bowl, "Turn it over." As the rocks poured out of the bowl, Stan asked him to judge how the bowl felt now that it was free of the burden of the rocks. The young men passed the empty bowl around the room as Stan read them a copy of the ancient saying.

Why don't you try this same exercise? Find a large empty bowl and a dozen rocks. Think about your last match and put a rock into the bowl for every incident that created frustration, disappointment, anger, or fear. Judge the heaviness of the rock-filled bowl. Do you want the burden of carrying that heavy bowl on the court as you play or live your life?

The next time you put a rock into your bowl of light because you're frustrated, angry, fearful, or thinking negatively, make a decision. Turn your bowl over by simply letting go of your toxic feelings. Allow the rocks to fall out. Then notice how quickly you feel good as your bowl fills up with perfect light. Don't you think it's time you clear away negative emotions and feelings from your bowl?

WHOOSH AWAY FRUSTRATION

You can **Whoosh!** away frustration in an instant. Imagine all of your frustration turning into two heavy rocks, one in each fisted hand. Exclaim aloud, **"Whoosh!"** and throw the rocks toward the floor and as far away from you as you can. There, the frustration is gone. Now with a bowl full of light, anything will be possible.

"Clearing" The Way To Victory

Can our inner game methods really help eliminate the destructive residue of the frustration you experience and free you to become the player you dream to be? It did for Kory Walter. Kory was the first middle hitter on Dave's 1996 team. Ask her and she'll tell you she believes that the **Clear** and **Reframing** techniques were contributing factors to the success of her senior season, but ask Dave and he'll tell you it wasn't an easy sell.

Kory was following in the footsteps of two straight All-State middle hitters and Dave needed her to step in and do the job. She had the ability to do so; however, the only problem was Kory had the reputation of being "her own worst enemy." Too many times she would let her frustration take control of her performance in crucial situations. Inconsistent as her play was, Kory stubbornly refused to employ any of the frustration management techniques of **Volleyball Cybernetics.** She flat-out didn't believe that the mental approach could help her game, that was until Kory's emotions got the best of her during an important early season match.

The Wildcats were playing the pre-season conference favorite, Firelands. After losing game one 14-16 in a heartbreaker, Kory and her teammates became unglued in game two and were routed 5-15. Kory was frustrated by the close loss in game one and it only got worse as game two progressed. For a team with hopes of winning the conference the night was a disaster.

The next day before practice Kory and her coach both agreed that she had let her emotions take control and ruin her performance. Dave explained that if the team was going to make a run at the conference championship, she was going to have to start controlling her frustration on the court instead of letting it control her! Still uncertain that Kory would respond to his advice, Dave decided to give Kory a rough draft of the chapter of this book on **How to Eliminate Frustration** and urged her to read it. But would she?

Kory and her teammates played much better over the next few weeks, winning five straight conference matches. The next match was the re-match with Firelands. If the Wildcats could defeat their rivals they would be in the driver's seat in the conference race! The match started out poorly for the Cats, especially for Kory. One hitting error became two, then three. Even though the rest of her game was fine, Dave knew his senior well enough to know her frustration level was on the rise. The Wildcats dropped game one by the same frustrating score as in the earlier match, 14-16. This time, however, things would be different. Kory cleared her frustration, made an adjustment in her game and started beating the Falcons with tips. Inspired by Kory's play, the rest of the team rose to the occasion and took games two and three 15-4, 15-13!

The rest of Kory's season was a dream come true. Her team won the conference championship and she received first team honors at the conference, county and district levels. She set the school record for kills in a season and was also named Player of the Year in the County. Best of all, Kory was named second team All-State, surpassing the honors of her predecessors!

The reason for her unexpected success? Kory will tell you, "I finally realized that getting mad at my mistakes was taking me out of my game. I decided that instead of taking my mistakes so seriously I would make light of them. If I hit a ball out of bounds there was no doubt in my mind the next hit would be a kill. Many times I would clear my mind between plays by thinking of something besides volleyball for a few seconds. I also reframed the very reason I was playing volleyball and stopped comparing myself to the great middle hitters before me. I decided to play volleyball, not to impress others, but because I loved the game."

Now that you have read about Kory's success story, what about yours? Who knows what a little **Clearing** and **Reframing** will do for your game?

It's time to learn how to achieve peak performance by tapping into the most resourceful state of mind athletes can experience… the **Power State.** Anchors away!

Chapter Nine

ANCHORING: HOW TO ACHIEVE THE POWER STATE

"The joy of surpassing the limits of the body is open to all."
Mihaly Csikszentmihalyi

Some call it **The Zone, Flow, Peak Performance, Optimal Experience, Wired, or On Automatic.** You can call it what you want, but unless you can consistently achieve this resourceful state of mind, you'll never tap the greatest quality of your inner resources. Athletes, coaches, and sports psychologists are constantly searching for ways to access this peak performance state of mind. This chapter is about how you can both capture and maintain the **Power State.**

Let's examine what you have learned so far. The first inner rule of performance is that your beliefs, self-talk, and body language control your state of mind. The second key rule is that your state of mind controls the level of your performance by controlling the way you feel. For instance, when you feel confident, focused, and composed, you finish plays. Feel unsure, distracted, and over-excited or under-excited and you major in below par performance.

If you are ever to achieve playing at your consistent best, you'll need to learn how to master the states of mind that control your feelings of confidence, concentration, and composure. Access all three of these dynamic states and you access the winning feeling you need to play your best. You also enter the **Power State of Mind.**

The irony is that you already know how to experience the **Power State.** Go into rewind and think about a time when you played at your best. Recall how you felt then and you'll know exactly how the **Power State** feels. Didn't you feel unstoppable with a tremendous feeling of certainty? Weren't your mind and body in perfect harmony? Weren't you totally absorbed in the here and now? You were in a **Power State.** There was no indecisiveness, second guessing, overtrying or frustration. Nothing could distract you. Aware of what was important and what wasn't, you were able to make the right decisions play after play. Game action seemed to be traveling at a slower speed. Your play was quick but unrushed. You had achieved the three sub-states of the **Power State: confidence, concentration, and composure.**

TAPPING IN: ANCHORING

There is no substitute for correct skill technique. We hope you understand that. Success in any endeavor requires skill development and repetition. However, you can learn and practice the proper serving technique all day long, but momentarily lose your confidence, focus, or composure, and even your most reliable serve to your favorite spot will find a way into the net. Your **Power State** becomes the **Stopper State!**

Thanks to the science of Neuro-Linguistic Programming (NLP), there is a way to automatically trigger these resourceful inner states that support your peak performance. The name of the NLP process is **Anchoring.** We briefly talked about anchoring in **Taking Action,** but let us further explain its power.

THE POWER OF ANCHORING

Since you started playing volleyball, you've had all kinds of experiences. Some good, some bad, and some even great! Each and every volleyball experience you've had, regardless of the outcome, has been stored in your biocomputer. Recorded along with these experiences was the state of mind you were in at the time. Thus, the experience and the state of mind are indelibly linked together.

Does this mean that if you retrieve the memory of one of your great volleyball moments, you also recall the associated state of mind? Yes, it does! Bet your destiny on it, too! Think of the full range of possibilities you have here. By using the NLP method of anchoring, you'll be able to generate any state of mind you want when you want it. Shank a pass, miss your first serve, or blow a spike attempt, and instead of your state of mind telling you what it wants you to do, you'll be telling it what you want it to do!

ANCHORS AWAY!

Anchoring is the process of reaching back in time to your past experiences and feelings of success and making those same positive feelings permanently available to your subconscious, thus allowing you to play as well, now, as you did then.

An anchor is any unique sight, sound, or feeling that is associated with an experience. An anchor can originate internally or externally, or be verbal or nonverbal. Anthony Robbins describes it this way: "Anytime you are in an intense emotional state, anything that occurs around you on a consistent basis while you are in that state becomes linked (anchored) to that state." The fact is you're always anchoring. Any time you play your favorite upbeat music in the locker room you're anchoring. Even the commercials you watch on TV base their effectiveness on the anchoring process. Advertisers spend millions creating unforgettable jingles or tunes and enlisting celebrities so that each time you hear the music or see the face of the celebrity, you're automatically conditioned to think of their product.

Anchor associations can be either positive or negative. For example, whenever you are in an intense negative state of mind, such as a feeling of frustration because you just blew an easy pass or hit a spike out of bounds, anything you're doing, seeing, and feeling becomes anchored to that state. Repeat these unique responses each time you get frustrated, and you reinforce the anchor. Specific facial, body, and verbal expressions, even your habit of breathing a certain way, all become permanently linked to the state you're experiencing.

Now, all you have to do to achieve a state of frustration is fire off several of your anchors linked to frustration and you will enjoy a conditioned response of frustration! Try this now while you're not frustrated and see for yourself. Just breathe the way you'd be breathing if you were frustrated; stand or sit the way you'd be standing or sitting if you were frustrated; whisper to yourself the same put-down expressions you normally recite whenever frustrated, add those uptight facial expressions and presto, you've successfully achieved a state of frustration!

ANCHORING FOR WINNING PERFORMANCE

Do you remember Pavlov's dogs? Pavlov wasn't known for his coaching talents, but he could have been. He knew how to train. If you remember your high school psychology, he was the scientist who conditioned dogs to salivate by ringing a bell. What he did was pure anchoring and great coaching! Every time he fed his dogs, he rang a bell. Then, the scientist rang the bell without giving the unsuspecting canines a drop of food, but the dogs salivated as if they were about to enjoy their favorite bowl of chow. Because the food was anchored to the sound of the bell, when they heard the bell, the dogs' nervous systems were programmed to expect food.

Apply this same anchoring formula to your game, and you will be able to experience a powerful state change any time you need one. All you have to do is fire off several word or hand action anchors, and you will experience the change you want just like Pavlov's dogs did! Here's how to do it!

1. Find a quiet place and a comfortable chair to sit in. Close your eyes and think back to a time when you were in the specific state of mind you want to anchor. If it's more confidence you're looking for, remember a game where you were unstoppable and incredibly confident. If it's concentration, think of a game where your mind and body were totally focused into the here and now. If it's more composure, think of a time when you felt poised and under complete control.

2. Step into the picture and experience the way you were feeling at the time of your success. At the peak of feeling confident, shout the word "Great!" as you slap your hands together. Enthusiastically fire off three powerful anchors one right after another in rapid succession. Make sure to coordinate the verbal ("Great!") and nonverbal (hands slap) action simultaneously.

87

3. Stack the anchor. Collect a bunch of them by recalling a series of winning moments and relive each one. At the very peak of feeling good, employ the same word and hand action and anchor three times consecutively. It's essential to upgrade your movie by projecting yourself inside the mental experience making it a first person event. Remember the way everything looked to you, how you felt and talked to yourself. Feel the intensity of the game and then anchor it all.

4. Time to test the positive anchor to see if you conditioned it into your mental computer. Get into a lousy frame of mind. Think about a game where you were messing it up big time. Recall several of your key miscues. Feel the embarrassment and sinking feeling you had at that unforgiving moment. Now fire off the positive anchor you just installed and test the conditioned response. Shout the word "Great!" three times as you forcefully slap your hands together. If you followed the anchoring procedures correctly, the anchor was effective. If it wasn't, review the process and start over. More reconditioning time is needed. Here's your anchoring checklist again:

- **Were you in an intense state?**
- **Did you anchor at the peak moment?**
- **Was the anchor unique?**
- **Did you stack the anchor often enough?**

STEPPING INSIDE THAT PROUD MOMENT

If you have trouble remembering a peak game in which you achieved a specific state you want anchored, there has to be a time, no matter how brief, when you performed aggressively or displayed exceptional poise or couldn't miss a spike. Relive any of these memorable moments and anchor it. The best way to access this proud moment is to follow this three-step process:

1. First, imagine the event as if you are observing it from a close camera angle.
2. Now, jump inside the picture and retrieve the rewarding moment from a first-person experience with one exception. Put all the action into a slow motion time frame. In this way you'll be able to **feel** the intensity of each crucial step of the successful action.
3. Finally, let your imagination go at game speed. Still in the first person, feel yourself performing the peak experience with the same pace of action as the original. Emphasize the intense **feeling** of the emotions you had at the time. Can you also retrieve the state of joy and satisfaction at the finish? Anchor it right now!

Just a word of caution. Effective anchors need to be enhanced and nurtured. Even if you create a strong positive anchoring response, make it a habit to anchor the state at least 10 times a day for 10 days. The best rule we know for permanent anchoring is — the more the better.

SPECIFIC ANCHORS

Here are some of the specific anchors we use at camp to lock in various states:

- **State of Confidence:**
  For Serving Success
  Verbal anchor. . . . . "Yes!"
  Nonverbal . . . . Snap fingers (one or both hands) or clench fist
  Play Success
  Verbal anchor. . . . . "Great!"
  Nonverbal . . . . Slap hands together

- **State of Concentration:**
  Pinpoint focus
  Verbal anchor. . . . . "Sight!" or "Ball!"
  Nonverbal . . . . Touch finger to right eye
  Peripheral Focus:
  Verbal anchor. . . . . "See!"
  Nonverbal . . . . Touch both eyes

- **State of Composure:**
  Aggressiveness
  Verbal anchor. . . . . "Beasts!" or "Big!"
  Nonverbal . . . . Fists of both hands extended below waist
  Toughness
  Verbal anchor. . . . . "Grit" or "Spunk" or "Brave"
  Nonverbal . . . . Right fist across chest
  Courage
  Verbal anchor. . . . . "Tough!"
  Nonverbal . . . . Extend both fists over head
  Calmness, Coolness, Poise
  Verbal anchor. . . . . "Ice!" or "Clear!"
  Nonverbal . . . . Press thumb against the second finger of the same hand (both hands)
  Smooth Play
  Verbal anchor. . . . . "Oil!"
  Nonverbal . . . . Squeeze both hands into a fist and release
  Optimism
  Verbal anchor. . . . . "Trust!"
  Nonverbal . . . . Slap right hand on right thigh

Feel free to create your own verbal and nonverbal anchors, the more unusual the better. Attach them to a state of mind which best supports the skills you're working to develop and enjoy the empowering state change. Your opponents won't!

ANCHOR BY MODELING

You can stack all kinds of anchors by modeling others. Observe the success of others in practice, matches, or on TV and anchor their winning moments.

> 1. Find someone who is performing well.
> 2. Using your senses of sight, sound, and feeling, go inside the winner and see, hear, and feel the internal emotions that are supporting the performance.
> 3. Intensify the internal state by firing off a strong anchor.
> 4. Anchoring winning performances must be practiced often.

Make it a habit to stay with one specific state by piling up at least a dozen similar anchoring experiences. For instance, if it's hitting confidence you're after, study a hitter on a roll and verbally anchor the hitter's inner emotions with the word "Yes!"

ANCHORING YOUR OWN BEST MOMENTS

Take advantage of your own great plays. Lock into the intense **Power State** you're in by immediately engaging a dramatic anchor. Then, when you need an emotional lift of confidence, concentration, or composure (after a mess-up or before a game), fire off that anchor several times.

Watch any Olympic event and you'll see the world's best athletes anchor themselves physically and verbally before and after their performance. Find a quiet way to anchor before, during, or after competition. The embarrassment you might feel by openly slapping your hands together and mumbling a word or two does not carry the same emotional discomfort as the rotten feeling you experience when playing poorly.

COACH MIKE GIBSON'S UNIQUE ANCHORING TECHNIQUE

Coach Mike Gibson uses a unique anchoring technique with his team. He credits the method for his team's success in winning tournaments and finishing higher than expected in others. Whenever his team wins a match, he immediately gets his team into a huddle and tells them:

"Take that great feeling that you have right now and put it into your right hand.

Squeeze it gently.

How does it feel?

What color is it?

That's right! (Whatever color and feeling a player expresses is good.)

Now put it in your pocket and hold on to it for safe keeping."

When the team gets into a tight spot and they need to break the other team's momentum, Mike asks his players, "How can the things in your pocket help you now?" He has them mentally pull out those great feelings and recall the exact way they felt when they first stored them. This can be done in a huddle as a team or individually during any break in the action.

After each successful game and match, Mike employs the anchoring procedure and suggests that each player add even more descriptive terms to her feelings. What texture does the good emotion have? How hot or cold is the feeling? Then when the game or match is on the line, the same procedure is repeated to pump up the team for the final push. "Squeeze your right hand and feel that winning feeling. Make it even bigger!" suggests Mike.

So start today to create those anchors that produce a **Power State** of mind. Stan talks about how he uses anchors to change his state of mind when needed. He often overcomes the disabling effects of fatigue, fear of speaking in front of large groups of people, brain-lock (in writing this book), and even a paralyzing fear of flying with the help of anchoring.

If you're ever on a plane that is experiencing rough weather, and you notice a smiling man furiously slapping his hands together and shouting the word "Great!" come on over and say hello to Stan.

Now let's take a close look at the master inner skill of concentration. It's the centerpiece of the **Power State.**

Chapter Ten

CONCENTRATION: HOW TO DEVELOP THE MASTER SKILL

"Concentration is the supreme art because no art can be achieved without it,
while with it, anything can be achieved."
Timothy Gallwey

YOUR FOCUSING DEVICE

The better you concentrate, the better you'll play. Underachievers show little control over their ability to focus attention on what is important and what isn't. Winners have learned to control and direct their attention skills. Without mastering this inner skill of concentration, success in any skill or activity is unlikely. A key to athletic excellence is the ability of the prime time athlete to pull all power of thought and desire on to a single task — to commit all energy to one act. In contrast, any outside element can distract the underachieving athlete.

Your focusing mechanism is your **Reticular Activating System.** Train it to work for you and you've taken a giant step towards becoming the player you dream of being. If you have trouble focusing in matches, practice, or the classroom, this chapter is for you. It's time to master the **Master Skill of Concentration.**

WHAT CONCENTRATION ISN'T

Concentration is not trying to push out thoughts, it is not analysis, and it is not contemplation. It is not thinking about the past or the future. Concentration isn't straining or trying hard to pay attention; it isn't gritting your teeth and tensing your muscles and using willpower.

Try too hard when serving, and you unintentionally increase muscle tension. Too much determination, or straining effort, decreases concentration and increases tension. Saying, "I will concentrate, I must concentrate," only makes it harder for you to prepare your body for optimal performance.

WHAT CONCENTRATION IS

Concentration is the art of focusing attention on a task, an object, an experience, or a goal. Concentration is a natural and effortless fundamental of the mind. Concentration means living in the present, in the **here and now.**

The past and future do not exist for athletes who have mastered this integral skill. For most athletes, unfortunately, the amount of time they can maintain quality concentration is all too brief.

HOW TO DEVELOP THE MASTER SKILL

There is no better way to improve your concentration than through the disciplined use of imagination. In all of the visualization exercises you've been asked to perform daily you're sharpening the master skill of the mind. In each exercise you are focusing your mental powers on an object, skill, or attitude.

Staying with a mental picture is the same as staying on the ball. The transition is natural. The systematic use of imagination will benefit you in so many other ways, as well. You will remember plays and become more aware of the entire court (peripheral vision). You will see the ball more clearly and it will appear larger. You will be able to listen to your coach's instructions during time-outs. No internal or external elements will distract you easily. You will perform and learn more effectively because you will be playing in the **here and now.**

Imagine what the effectiveness of a flashlight would be if there were no aluminum reflector inside its head. The light would diffuse in all directions. When you fail to concentrate, your mental power is weakened in the same way.

THE TWO KINDS OF CONCENTRATION

To be successful you need to develop two forms of concentration:

1. **Pinpoint or narrow concentration**
2. **Peripheral or wide range (broad) concentration**

Both forms can be improved with our cybernetic programming methods.

1. PINPOINT CONCENTRATION

When you focus attention completely on the ball while serving, blocking, or passing, you are exercising pinpoint concentration. The advantage of pinpoint concentration is that it prevents two purposes or goals from occupying your mind at the same time.

You already know that when your focus wanders during competition you're in trouble. For example, when you are at the serving line ready to execute a crucial serve, if your eyes and mind momentarily stray from the ball, you can expect less than your best serve. There are many distractions that diffuse serving concentration: thinking about your last missed serve, the importance of the serve after looking up at the scoreboard, becoming aware of the crowd, or being engrossed in the actions of teammates, coaches, opponents, or officials. If you seriously want to become a prime time player, you need to eliminate interference and totally center the power of your focus on the job at hand.

DEVELOPING PINPOINT CONCENTRATION

A simple way to increase your ability to concentrate is to see how long you can hold on to a single thought in your mind... any thought. This can be done any place and any time. Right now, for instance, see how long you can hold on to the thought running through your mind. Or else, think of the number one. Hold on to the image of the number one as long as you can. At the beginning, you will be able to stay with the image for only a few seconds. Practice this simple routine a few times a day, and you will be surprised how quickly you can increase your ability to concentrate. Whenever your mind begins to wander away from the thought, gently bring your mind back to it. Never force your concentration. Unhurriedly return your attention to the original thought.

To continue practicing concentration you simply need an object on which to center your attention. A volleyball is as good an object as any. Concentrate on this image on your inner screen in bed each night and morning. Remember to vividly detail the ball for a few minutes. Gently focus your complete attention on the image of the ball, becoming totally engrossed in its beauty. Develop a fascination, even a love for the ball. Observe its natural beauty. Begin to feel that you are becoming one with the ball. You and the ball are one. The ball is an extension of your hand. As you are observing the ball, say to yourself, **"Ball, Ball, Ball."** As you hold this picture in your mind, you are seeing, feeling, experiencing, and recording the ball into the memory banks of your mind. You are also developing your power of concentration.

2. PERIPHERAL CONCENTRATION

Peripheral vision, on the other hand, is total court awareness. Your ability to observe the movements of your teammates around you, while at the same time being aware of the position of the ball, is essential to your performance. When on defense, if you simply pay strict attention to either your opponent or the ball, you may find yourself out of position. If you want to be an effective setter, developing your peripheral vision is a must. Unfortunately too much pinpoint concentration can develop into tunnel vision, which is great for serving or focusing on the ball, but handicaps your court awareness. To play good defense or to attack your opponents' defensive weaknesses, it is essential to be aware of the movement of the ball, your teammates, and your opponents — all at the same time.

We are not suggesting that peripheral concentration is a substitute for verbal communication among teammates. **TALK, TALK, TALK** on the court is a must! You can never communicate too much with your teammates. How many times have you or a teammate failed to verbally communicate and ended up messing up the play because you were unaware of the position of others on the court? Peripheral concentration helps you make aggressive plays, especially when your teammate forgets to communicate verbally.

ALTERNATING CONCENTRATION

Want to dramatically improve your level of play? **Improve your ability to effectively switch between one form of concentration and the other.**

During the continuing action of a volleyball game your focus bounces back and forth hundreds of times between pinpoint and peripheral vision. Take, for example, a simple segment of a rally, and observe how many times one player employs instant changes of concentration. The player reads the force of an incoming ball (pinpoint), moves to get into position (peripheral), makes the pass (pinpoint), reads the flight of the ball (pinpoint), the movements of his/her teammates (peripheral), moves into proper position for the upcoming attack (peripheral), makes the correctly timed approach to the ball (peripheral), then jumps, swings, and hits the ball (pinpoint).

Want to enjoy more success on the court? You will, as soon as you learn how to improve your ability to shift concentration gears. What if we could show you how to improve your ability to alternate your concentration through a few simple exercises? Would that help?

SEEING OUT OF YOUR EARS

Oh! You can't see out of your ears? That's too bad, because if you could, you would be able to move more effectively on the court. Think of it. You could read the opponent's attack with your eyes and see your teammates with your ears!

Do this and see if you can see out of your ears:

- Look straight ahead and place both hands behind your head.
- Focus on any object directly in front of you. With two fingers up, start moving your hands around toward the front of your head.
- As soon as you can see (peripherally) the extended finger on each hand, stop the movement of your hands. Remember, your eyes are staring straight ahead.

By now your hands should be somewhere near your ears. Imagine that your ears are doing the identifying, not your eyes. Wiggle different fingers and identify your moving fingers using your ears only.

See, we told you! You can see out of your ears.

ON-THE-COURT DRILLS FOR ALTERNATING CONCENTRATION

DRILL ONE: SQUARE-UP DRILL

Try this Pinpoint-Peripheral Alternating Exercise with three of your friends. Employed daily at camp, the **Square-Up Drill** opens up the court for the narrowly focused player.

- The drill requires four players to form a circle and join hands. They drop hands and take two big steps backward forming a square. Each athlete faces a partner who is standing directly opposite.
- Each player is flanked by an athlete to her immediate right and left.
- On the command, **"Pinpoint,"** each athlete in the square focuses on the right eye of the player standing directly in front of her for several seconds.
- On the command, **"Peripheral,"** each athlete raises one hand high over her head.
- Still looking straight ahead with a softer stare, all players must identify which hand is being raised by the player to both sides.
- The identification process must be accomplished without looking to the right or left. **The ears are doing the peripheral seeing.** The eyes of the four athletes must remain **"soft"** centered straight ahead during the entire drill.
- The drill continues back and forth between the pinpoint and peripheral commands until the players are able to comfortably recognize the upraised hands **seeing only with their ears.**

With practice and a little imagination, ears are conditioned to see with 20/20 vision! The next step is to use two volleyballs in the drill.

- The head couple has a ball which they pass back and forth to each other, as the side couple pass to each other at the same time.
- Using a mix of overhead and forearm passes, the purpose of the drill is to see how long the four players can pass their balls across to their partners without the two balls colliding or hitting the floor.
- Eyes are used to pass and ears are used to read the peripheral action of the side couple.

DRILL TWO: FINDING THE LINE

- With a ball and a partner (or by yourself using a wall), move to an open area on the court.
- Find a line on the floor that you can easily locate and focus your attention on.
- Set the ball about 10-12 feet high above your head and immediately find the "line" you've chosen.
- As soon as you find your "line," quickly look to find the ball again and set it once more.
- Again, immediately find your line and then quickly look to find the ball so you can set it again.
- See how many times you can successfully alternate your concentration and keep the ball in the air.
- Set a goal to improve that number — then work to achieve it.

This drill can also be done using the forearm pass.

DRILL THREE (WITH A PARTNER): HOW MANY FINGERS?

- Stand facing your partner, about ten feet apart from each other.
- Have your partner toss a ball that you can set.
- As soon as the toss is made, your partner holds a hand in front of her chest and displays a certain number of fingers.
- Quickly look to your partner and yell out the number of fingers your partner is holding up — then quickly look to find the ball and set it back.
- As soon as you set the ball, hold up a number of fingers for your partner to find before the ball is set back to you.
- Keep it going as long as you can!

Set a goal of how many times in a row you and your partner can successfully return the ball while reading the finger count. When the score is reached set a higher one. With time don't be surprised at how much better your vision is in competition. You'll also notice that you're rarely out of position and no longer running into teammates.

DRILL FOUR (WITH PARTNER):

A gymnastics mat is needed for this drill.

- Place the mat lengthwise between your partner and yourself.
- Do a forward roll on the mat, moving in the direction of your partner.
- As you complete the forward roll, have your partner toss a ball in your direction.
- Regain your feet, find the ball and forearm pass it to a pre-determined target.

This drill can also be done using a backward roll and/or using an overhead pass.
Safety Tip: Because of possible dizziness, never repeat this drill more than six times in a row.

HOW TO DEVELOP THE SKILL OF ALTERNATING CONCENTRATIONS AT HOME

DRILL ONE:

It's easy. Select three different objects in the room in which you are sitting; a bookshelf is excellent for this exercise. Use the middle book and the two end books as the three objects upon which to center your attention. Focus on the middle book. Select a distinguishing mark on this book and center your attention on it for a few seconds. Now change your focus from narrow to broad. While staring at the middle book, see if you can become visually aware of the two books placed at each end of the shelf. Repeat this alternating exercise many times.

DRILL TWO: THE RUSSIANS ARE COMING

In the book *Red Gold* (1988), Grigori Raiport describes several techniques used in the Soviet Olympic training program to improve an athlete's ability to alternate concentration. Each of the following should be mastered before moving on to the next one:

- Get two radios. Place one about five feet to your left and the other the same distance to your right. Tune to two different stations and adjust the volume equally to a pleasant, moderate level. Sit between the radios with your eyes closed. Visualize your attention as a beam of light coming from your forehead. Alternate your attention back and forth every twenty seconds from one radio to the other by snapping your fingers. Do this exercise five minutes daily until you reach the goal of being able to concentrate totally on one station while "tuning out" the other.

- Read a book while the news is on the radio. Alternate your attention for about twenty seconds each between reading and listening, and then try to become oblivious to what you are reading while you are listening and vice versa. Do this for at least five minutes every day until you reach your objective: total concentration on reading to the total exclusion of the news.

- Learn to become an introvert by imagining turning the beam of your attention inward. While the news is still on the radio, start subtracting in your mind the number 7 from 100. Do this exercise daily until you can become oblivious to the news while subtracting.

The degree of volleyball success you experience will be in exact proportion to how well you focus your attention on the task at hand. No more and no less. So how much time are you willing to spend on developing and maintaining the "master skill"? How badly do you want to become a winner?

Chapter Eleven

COMPOSURE: THE ART OF "LET IT HAPPEN" AND "MAKE IT HAPPEN"

"Nature functions with effortless ease and carefreeness. When we harness these forces, we create success and good fortune with effortless ease."

Deepak Chopra

Without the proper mixture of aggressive effort and poise, playing at your best is difficult, if not impossible. Defensively, play should be hard and spirited — a **make it happen** mindset. Offensively, a relaxed frame of mind that produces a more consistent, less rushed style of play is preferred — a **let it happen** focus. You're about to learn how to regulate your intensity level so it serves you best at all times on the court, including when the match is on the line. Success requires controlling the composure meter of your mind and body. When it comes time to play the athlete who masters his emotions, feelings, and arousal effort more often ends up in the winner's locker room.

PLAYING UPTIGHT

Playing uptight can be caused by many factors, most of which you can regulate. Let's examine the principal reasons for tight performance. Then we'll offer you some cybernetic solutions.

1. **You try too hard.** There's too much effort. You perform under the impression that the harder you struggle, the better you'll do. How wrong you are!
2. **You worry about making mistakes.** The fear of making a mistake inhibits your performance. Muscles are tighter. Your play is mechanical and tentative.

3. **You are overly concerned** about the outcome of the game or the outcome of the play. The result is careful, anxious, and mechanical play.

4. **You are overly aroused and overly excited.** You forgot that your best game was spontaneous and natural. Becoming overly aroused strains the success mechanism. You feel that every action is a life and death struggle. You become so anxious to do the right thing, so conscious of every move, that your performance is tense.

Unfortunately, most coaches have no systematic strategy for training their players in the art of **hanging loose** in games. In fact, these are the same coaches who unwittingly produce uptight players for big games by being uptight and overly aroused themselves.

After studying various mind/body relaxation techniques and exercises, we found that some work better than others. Depending on the individual, what applies for one can be quickly rejected by another. You decide which methods and exercises you feel most comfortable doing.

If you're a coach who shouts, **"Relax! Relax!"** before your players serve, please read this chapter more than once.

HOW TO OVERCOME A LACK OF CONFIDENCE AND TOO MUCH EFFORT

Stop trying so hard. You don't have to go at full speed to perform at top speed. You don't have to kill yourself to be a winner. When you try too hard, you upset the balance between the doing and thinking, and between your success mechanism and your body. In the end, muscle fights muscle. Every time you exert extra effort while executing a skill, speed and agility are lost.

Physically this is what happens: Each time there is a precise body motion there is a coordination between two sets of muscles. Muscles can only pull a bone in one direction. Due to the force of contraction, the muscles that are designed to pull the bone in the opposite direction, the antagonistic muscles, have to relax and let go. Whenever you try too hard, the protagonistic muscles responsible for pulling the bone function perfectly, but the antagonistic muscles have difficulty relaxing since they are tense from the over effort. The resulting action is muscle tying up muscle.

If you try too hard when passing, don't you find the pass off target much too often? If you try too hard to set a ball, you suddenly find your hands lacking the necessary softness and control. Fingers seem to lose their quick reflexes. Too often the set is released with double contact or is again simply off target. When hitting, you may notice your armswing is less smooth. Instead of swinging freely through the ball, your arm jerks back after making contact.

THE IMPORTANCE OF REDUCING OVER EFFORT

Learn from this lesson: Clench your hands as many times as you can within five seconds. Have someone else time the five seconds for you. Score a point for each clench. Make every clench intense and full. You're going for the World Hand Clenching Championship Trophy, so get excited and really pump out those clenches. 100% effort...no 90% trying. Ready, count!

1 second...2 seconds...3 seconds...4 seconds...5 seconds...Stop!

Remember your count? Now we want you to do it again, but this time reduce the intense effort just a bit. Be quicker if you can, but don't try so hard. Ready...count!

1 second...2 seconds...3 seconds...4 seconds...5 seconds...Stop!

Got your new score? Was it higher on the second attempt? Most athletes at camp score higher when they employ less effort. Why? Blame your faithful subconscious. When you overtry your subconscious takes you at your word that you're going for a world record, and sends instructions to too many muscles. Muscles that should be relaxing are contracting, resulting in muscle fighting muscle. Both antagonistic and protagonistic muscles are contracting at the same time, producing less speed and more fatigue.

Athletes often score higher when they reduce their effort because there is no muscle tie-up. The antagonistic muscles are allowed to relax and the protagonistic muscles are allowed to do their job of pulling. It's a concept you must understand and accept, because your overtrying effort is inhibiting your game.

A MASTER CONCEPT FOR CONTROLLING YOUR COMPOSURE: PLAYING AT SPEEDS

How would you like to have a composure control knob for speed, intensity, and poise? You could if you're willing to evaluate your performance effort just for awhile with a 1 to 10 rating scale. Start by considering an **overtry effort** as a 10 speed reading. A 9 speed would require a slight effort reduction. Half speed effort would qualify you for a 5 speed. Got it?

When you reduced your effort in the hand clenching exercise from a 10 to 9, for example, didn't your performance level improve? Try reducing the intensity effort a number or two during some of your drills or games. You may find yourself finishing more plays and playing with more composure. Track coaches have discovered that when they ask their sprinters to reduce their intensity effort, ever so slightly, their running times improve.

Play our number game of **less is more** and see if you're not quicker to the ball or serving better.

LEARN TO TRUST YOURSELF

When it's time to play, it is totally up to you to trust yourself and remain composed. For the athlete who understands the laws of cybernetics, trusting yourself means trusting your **God-given** creative success mechanism. **Letting it happen** means the same as **letting it work.** Attempting to make your subconscious operate as a success mechanism through extra effort only strains your mechanism. An overtrying effort is self-defeating. The words **trust** and **let** are synonymous with maximum performance. Since your creative mechanism operates below the conscious level, it is essential that you always place a positive demand upon it. The best way you can do that is by developing an expectancy to do well or **a winning feeling.**

Whenever you experience that winning feeling, your internal machinery is automatically set for success. There is no need for worry, fear, or anxiety about the outcome of the next play or the match. When that winning feeling is strong, you're in a **Power State.** Your attacking skills are in an incredible groove. You feel stronger and quicker. You can do no wrong. Your play is creative, spontaneous, and free. Performance is automatic, natural, and effortless. How do you attain that magical winning feeling? Again, our secret is simply to recapture in memory the feeling of success and confidence from a past peak experience. Every athlete at one time has had a peak match or game when he or she could do no wrong. Can you remember yours? As soon as you do, **VAK it for future use!**

GETTING LOOSE BEFORE THE GAME

Here are several coaching guidelines you can consider to keep yourself loose and cool before games.

1. **Winning does not have to be expressed as a stated goal.** Winning is the benefit of playing your best. Think about the game as an opportunity to learn and grow. Remind yourself that the fun is in the process of preparing and playing and not in the result alone. There are many difficult challenges and responsibilities in this world; playing in a volleyball game is not one of them. Today's game is tomorrow's trivia. The importance of the game is an illusion whose outcome will be quickly forgotten. The effort you and your coaches expend to be the best you can is the real part of the process and carries the most lasting impact!

2. **Never over — or underestimate your opponents.** A well-prepared team is one that understands the opponents' strengths and weaknesses. A good defensive strategy is to shut down the opponents' number one or two offensive players. The opposition may win the game, but their star players are not going to have an easy time contributing. That's a strategy we both follow as coaches. The basic defensive strategy is to keep the ball away from the best hitters as much as possible and make them work harder to get good attack opportunities. This forces their less talented players to step up to win the game.

3. **It's important that you trust yourself, trust your teammates, and trust your coach.** Belief in all three is necessary for a successful outcome. Everything that you or your coach does in practice should be designed to develop and perpetuate this trust. How many times have you observed a team who wins a summer league championship fail miserably during the regular season because they didn't believe in their coach's ability. Believe in yourself, your teammates, and especially believe in your coach.

4. **In the pre-game locker room session recognize the importance of "giving."** Suggest this to your coach: Each player (coaches and managers included) stands up and describes to the team a good deed that he or she has performed that day for someone other than a teammate. This is some unselfish and helpful act that contributes to improving the life of someone (parents, teachers, friends, even a passer-by) — anything from cleaning the kitchen, washing Dad's car, helping someone do her homework, or running an errand for

Mom or a teacher. As the season progresses you'll find the good deed stories will become more generous and noble. One of the goals of good coaching and playing is to see the bigger picture... **the value of giving and sharing both on and off the court.** The act of selfishness is one of life's most disempowering strategies contrasted with the act of contribution as life's most rewarding. The choice is yours. There are too many self-serving people of all ages living lives with the habit of taking without discovering the higher reward of giving. Too bad for the people around them, and worse yet, too bad for themselves and their team. Isn't volleyball a game of **"giving"**?

Have you done a good deed for someone today? What was it?

HANGING LOOSE THE NIGHT BEFORE THE MATCH

1. The night before your next match try this at home. Sit down in a comfortable chair or lie down in bed and go to the movies in your mind. Defense first. Visualize yourself executing your assignments for the approaching match. If your responsibility is to play the crosscourt power angle, watch yourself confidently acting out your assignment by digging up a ball that the opponent's big hitter slams at you. Watch yourself read a tip and step into the middle and pass it right to the setter. See yourself reacting to a weak side hit that deflects off the block in front of you by diving in and picking it up before it gets to the floor. See yourself take a down ball and pass it to the setter. Then jump into the movie and feel yourself performing these same outstanding actions.

2. For offensive visualization, picture your team destroying your opponent's defense, finding open holes, beating the block, and putting the ball to the floor with poise and confidence. See yourself driving the ball past the block and to the floor again and again. Watch yourself serve tough serves for aces. Now take the movie to the next step and jump into the action. Feel yourself executing the specific assignment that your coach expects from you. Remember, you get what you expect!

No, our teams didn't win every match. But most of the time they were ready to. Coach, prepare your team to be physically and mentally peaked for the match. That should be your main goal for practices before match day. Then enjoy their joy of competing. What more would you want from them and what more would you want from yourself?

HANGING LOOSE DURING THE MATCH

Whenever you perform poorly or need a mental uplift, use the confidence-inducing anchors you've been developing and fire a couple off. During a break in the action you can combine the anchoring with a short stint of visualization. For example, you suddenly lose your passing touch. Wait for a stop in the action and get back into a confident groove by creating half a dozen imaginary passes in the direction of the setter's head. Reinforce the imaginary successes by reciting your favorite verbal anchor word for passing (Ball!) along with your favorite physical anchor (the hand action of snapping your fingers) with each mental pass.

Anchoring is one of the most powerful techniques for changing states. Be smart and use anchors.

Here are the full range of **Volleyball Cybernetics** mind and body relaxation training procedures. These exercises practiced on a daily basis are designed to reduce tension, unclutter the mind from extraneous and disturbing thoughts, increase concentration, and eliminate the growing feeling of anxiety before or during the match.

1. The quickest and simplest of the muscle relaxing methods is called the **breathing technique.** This technique can be used at any time, even on the serving line. It takes only a few seconds. Natural breathing is a universal rhythm. By listening to the air pass evenly through the mouth and nose, relaxation can be quickly obtained. Silently repeat, "Let go," on each exhalation. Letting go implies the releasing of muscle tension.

2. The second relaxation exercise is based on Dr. Edmund Jacobson's famous method for decreasing tension before sleep. Used before matches, it will decrease tension. Lying in bed or sitting in a chair, slowly count to ten, increasing (not decreasing) your entire body's tension on each upward count. After reaching ten start counting backwards gradually decreasing your body's tension. All tension is fully released by the count of one. If you don't feel completely relaxed at the count of one, repeat the exercise again. While counting forward squeeze your toes and buttocks, clench your fists, and grit your teeth tighter on each count. As you count backwards allow these same parts to go limp and loose.

3. The deflating ball technique is a quickie that can be used in the locker room or on the bench. Close your eyes, take a deep breath, and slowly exhale. Begin to visualize yourself as an inflated volleyball gradually losing its air. As the air escapes from your mouth (the valve), let your body go slack, wiggle your neck, and allow your head to limply land on your chest. In less than ten seconds, you've become a deflated ball.

4. The light-gray cloud technique helped one of the worst hotheads Stan has ever coached stay cool in games. The player was one of his better players, but once an official's call went against him the player would become enraged and useless to his team. Nothing his teammates or Stan could say would calm him down. The athlete tried several visualization techniques but nothing helped. What finally worked for him was the light-gray cloud technique. If you qualify for "the hothead of the month" award, try this the next time life treats you unfairly.

    Imagine the official blowing the whistle and making a horrible call against you. Instead of getting upset and feeling smoke emanating from every orifice of your body, imagine a cool, light gray cloud protecting your body. The bothersome call cannot penetrate this cool, gray shield and upset you. You're totally protected and insulated! You are free to stay calm, cool, and collected. Press your thumb and second finger together to anchor this great feeling of control. Now, when you are confronted with a "bad call," quickly place these two fingers together for instant recall of your cool, light gray cloud.

5. The quiet room technique will aid you in quieting your mind, while at the same time relaxing your body. Quieting the mind requires slowing down the thinking process. Before the match it's a good idea to still your mind with a brief two-minute break. Build a little

mental quiet room in your imagination. Paint the walls of this perfect, peaceful, and comfortable room in your favorite color. Mentally construct the walls with thought-proof and sound-proof materials. In the middle of the room, imagine your favorite easy chair. Whenever you feel pre-match tension mounting, mentally retire into this quiet center to relax and clear your mind. Visualize yourself sitting down in your chair totally at ease and feeling secure.

Escaping into your quiet room has the effect of clearing your creative mechanism. Just as an electronic adding machine can be cleared of previous computations with the pressing of a key, you can clear your mental machinery of life's unwanted computations by escaping to your quiet room.

6. The blackboard technique attacks those concerns that in reality you can't do anything about. It can be anything from a lack of rapport with a certain teammate who refuses to appreciate your talents, to a coach who doesn't appreciate the best in you. Every time you think about them (probably it's much too often), a feeling of hopelessness sets in.

Would you like to regain control of your thoughts and stop wasting good energy on bad thoughts? Do this:

Feel yourself sitting in your mental quiet room. There is a chalkboard in front of you. Picture the numbers 1, 2, and 3 boldly written on the board. Look at the board and notice that your three most energy-absorbing concerns are clearly written out next to the numbers. Next to the number one is your most important concern. Become part of this movie and feel yourself getting up from the chair and walking over to the board. Pick up the eraser on the runner below the board and erase the number one concern. Wipe it off completely. There, it's gone forever. You've eliminated it from your mind. Do you feel the relief? Realize that the bothersome thought cannot annoy you anymore, because it's no longer in your mind. You're the one who put it there and now you erased it. That was easy. Return to your chair and stare at the second concern until you grow tired of looking at it. It's brought you enough pain. What are you going to do? You can't resolve it, but you can prevent it from draining your energy. You know what you have to do. The eraser is still in your hand. Stand up and purposefully walk over to the board. Erase your second concern permanently and completely. Now, it too is gone. Nice job! Return to your chair and think about your final concern on the board. Hasn't it brought you enough grief? Let's get rid of it...now! Walk over and erase it from your life.

Hey! Congratulations! There are no concerns left unless you want to put them back on your mental chalkboard. That is your privilege. Whenever you want something to bother you, just jot it down on your inner chalkboard in bold print and keep thinking about it. Do you really want to waste energy worrying about an area of concern that you can't do anything about, except worry? I don't think you do. You know what has to be done. Use that mental eraser and get on with your life and your season.

7. Garbage in...garbage out! It's essential to keep your self-talk positive. How many times do we have to tell you? When you talk, your automatic pilot is listening. Here are some affirmative action expressions that will help you stay in the groove:

Hang tough...

Let go...

Stay loose...

Relax...

Let it happen (on offense)...

Make it happen (on defense)...

Forget it...

Trust is a must...

Tomorrow's another day...

Just do it...

8. From Olympians to professional athletes, a growing number of athletes have been using a mental procedure called Transcendental Meditation (TM) to quiet their minds and energize their bodies. They claim it helps them think clearly, feel relaxed, and perform better. Believe them! It does!

Dr. Herbert Benson has written a book called *The Relaxation Response*. This best seller prescribes a simple meditation technique that is based on the TM procedure. It's easy to learn and results in a deeper level of relaxation compared to our other relaxation techniques. Judge for yourself. All you'll have to do is close your eyes, pay attention to your breathing, and silently repeat a meaningless one syllable word or sound to yourself. Follow these instructions:

- Sit quietly in a comfortable chair.
- Close your eyes.
- Deeply relax all muscles, beginning at your feet and progressing up to your face.
- Breathe through your nose and become aware of your breathing rhythm. As you do, repeat the word "one" each time you exhale.
- Continue for 10 to 20 minutes.
- When you're finished, sit quietly for several minutes at first with your eyes closed, then with your eyes open. When distracting thoughts occur, ignore them, not through effort, but by repeating the sound "one." Practice the technique once or twice daily.

Dr. Benson believes that this method helps the individual cope with the pressures of society and competition. Try it yourself and observe the outcome.

GETTING A GOOD NIGHT'S SLEEP

Stan has often been asked, "Is there a method of mentally training an athlete to fall asleep?" Coaches realize the importance of getting a good night's rest for their players and themselves in order to be in top shape for practice or a match. A sleepless night robs you of your energy. Counting sheep seems to be the only solution coaches offer their players to solve the problem of a sleepless night. A common cause of sleeplessness usually is an overactive mind filled with worry, excitement, and anxiety. This is Stan's favorite **"let it happen"** strategy to quiet his mind, relax his body, and most of all, give him a good night's sleep. He begins by slowing down all the action of the people in his thoughts to a slow motion time frame. All conversation and body movement, including his own, are reduced to a crawl. Words are slurred. People are tired and yawning. Sleep soon arrives.

Here's another method: The next time you have trouble sleeping, get into a comfortable position in bed. Close your eyes and concentrate on your breathing. Every time you exhale feel the air pass through the space below your nose. Pay careful attention to the air as it passes through this space for several minutes. Now look upward behind your closed eyelids toward the top of your head. Hold this eye position for as long as you can. When your eyes become tired, let them drop to their natural position. Again return to the rhythm of your breathing. This time silently say to yourself, "Relax" on each exhalation. Starting with your toes feel the tension release from each part of your body, progressing upward. Think of the muscle, then the joint above it. Continue upwards. Consider all parts of your body... even your teeth, nose, eyebrows, temple, scalp, and finally hair. Sleep will arrive sooner than you think. If you find yourself still awake, repeat the cycle, starting from the feet again.

By centering your mind on your breathing rhythm, your mind is pacified. Two thoughts cannot occupy the mind at the same time. By listening to your rhythmic breathing, you will find yourself drifting away from your active thoughts. Your body will lose its tension, and a deeper level of body comfort will be experienced followed by a natural and rewarding sleep. Sweet dreams.

THE CHOICE IS YOURS

Employ one technique for concentration and composure or employ several. Knowing how to concentrate and play cool are the keys to a better game. You cannot instruct yourself through willpower to concentrate and relax. The effective way is to train these responses into your biocomputer with repetition. So start training.

Chapter Twelve

The Winner's Mind In The Game

"Flow with whatever may happen and let your mind be free:
Stay centered by accepting whatever you are doing. This is the Ultimate."
Chuang-Tzu

Once competition begins, your automatic mind takes over. There is little conscious thinking involved. Usually, your actions are not thought out while you perform. Calculation and visualization take place in practice, in the locker room, on the bench, or at home, but rarely in the game. Think too much while playing and your play is mechanical and tentative. Successful play is automatic, flowing, and spontaneous. **The play is the thing**. The athlete who thinks while doing is interfering with the doing. In competition winners know how to...

- let go of the past
- let it happen
- stop trying so hard
- stop thinking
- relax
- go with the flow
- just do it... and trust themselves.

It's the successful athlete who has learned not to jam the creative machinery while playing. Think back. Weren't your best matches automatic, uninhibited, and unthinking? Ask the best volleyball player you know what he or she thinks during a match. "I don't know!" or "Nothing" will probably be the answers. It's the underachiever who does the thinking during the match.

You don't need the advice of a sports psychologist or Yogi Berra telling you, "You can't think and hit at the same time." Once the match begins, highly complex motor skills such as hitting, serving, or passing are performed automatically. Because they are actions that are classified as overlearned skills, they are handled on the subconscious (automatic) level.

YOUR MIND STAYS AHEAD OF THE ACTION

Largely because of the speed of the action and a kaleidoscopic flow of changing situations, your mind has to stay ahead of your body's action. Any skill that has to be thought about is destined to fail. The skill that has to be deliberated upon is not ready for competitive use.

You perform with less certainty when you have to consciously think about the position of your elbow on your armswing or which foot is forward on the defensive stance. Skill in any performance arena, whether in sports, playing the piano, or typing, is directed by your habitmaker, the subconscious mind.

SEARCHING FOR PLAYING CLUES

What would happen to the performance level of a skilled typist if she suddenly became aware of the specific movements of her fingers as she typed? She'd probably make more mistakes than usual and type more slowly. The typist's mind, like the athlete's mind, has to be ahead of her body actions so that she can continually pick up words from the dictation. Likewise, the volleyball player's mind has to be focused ahead searching for the cues and clues of the on-going action of the match.

When you are in the middle of a long, exciting rally, you don't look at the ball as you approach the set from the outside and think, "Time to get my off-hand up to help sight the ball." Your mind has to stay well ahead of the action, searching for the critical playing cues, such as the position of the blockers or the holes in the defense to shoot for. All good players have the ability to approach, jump, and spike the ball, while at the same time spontaneously analyzing the fast forming playing cues that are essential and deleting those that aren't. Without a clear and flowing mind you will not be able to play good volleyball.

PROOF THAT TOO MUCH THINKING STINKS

Your responsibility is to keep your game on automatic control during competition. Try this demonstration with a friend who is a great server. Ask her to serve 10 serves to her favorite spot. Then ask her to explain her serving secrets. Is it her follow through and relaxed wrist action? Or is it her perfect toss? Ask her to tell you which foot she prefers to rest her weight on before starting to serve. Keep pumping her with thought provoking questions. After she reveals her secrets ask her to serve ten more balls. More often than not you'll find her serving percentage and accuracy will decrease. Why? With your devious guidance, she moved her serving skill from an unthinking, automatic level to a thinking conscious level.

Try complimenting the opponents' best hitter during an appropriate break in the action at the net and see what happens. Pay your respects to her perfect armswing, her leaping ability, or her ability to find the holes in your team's defense. Your acclaim can get her to think about her great hitting ability and in the process change an automatic skill to manual control. If she falls for it, you've got her!

Coaches, how many times have you experienced the following scenario? You're moving about the gym during a practice or summer camp. You stop to watch someone's next attempt to serve, hit, or set, and the player makes an error. When you offer feedback, she replies, "I only do that when you're watching," or "That's the first time I've messed up."

What the player is really saying is, "I thought about really doing well that time, Coach, because you were watching." The player took the skill from the unthinking level to the thinking or trying level, wanting to do it perfectly in front of the coach. The bottom line is that the athlete tightened up and didn't perform the skill like she could otherwise.

Dave has a close coaching friend at a rival school in his conference, who unknowingly used this powerful expectancy factor against Dave's team for years. It worked until Dave figured it out. No matter who had the stronger team, the Elyria West Wolverines would defeat Dave's Keystone Wildcats' squad. The losing streak reached into double digits. There were times when Keystone would play poorly and there were times when Dave's Keystone team played well, only to fall to an amazing West comeback.

After each Elyria West win Dave's friend would find a way to sincerely praise the frustrated Wildcats. "You guys played great! That's the best I've ever seen a Keystone team play. You didn't make any mistakes," he would say. The compliments continued with each loss. The unintentional psyche job was sending a subconscious message that good wasn't good enough and that playing perfectly was the only way to defeat Elyria West. With the advent of Volleyball Cybernetics into Dave's coaching, Dave began to realize what his friend had done. His friend had complimented Dave's team on a conscious level but at the same time insulted the team's talent on a subconscious level. Did Dave's team eventually defeat their conference rival? What do you think?

With an attitude adjustment and a lot of hard work, Dave's Wildcats ended the seventeen match home court winning streak of the Wolverines with a thrilling three-game victory. Since that exciting night the Wildcats have beaten the Wolverines nine of the last twelve meetings. Why? Surely many factors are involved, but Dave's girls learned that they didn't have to play perfectly to win. All they had to do was stop thinking, trust themselves, and go out and **just do it.**

THE "CUMULATIVE POSITIVE MIND SET" OR HOW TO DEVELOP THE WINNER'S INSTINCT FOR MAKING CORRECT DECISIONS

Have you noticed that winning coaches seem to possess an innate ability to make decisions in competition that pan out? These coaches, when confronted with a situation that calls for action, seem to instinctively know what to do. While others often have difficulties making winning decisions under the same circumstances. Given the incredible creative ability of the subconscious serving us, why don't we all experience its full inventive benefits?

Why do some coaches instinctively substitute poorly or make the incorrect crunch time strategy decisions? Our cybernetic explanation for their dilemma: too much negative thinking for too long a time. They have never learned how to set their subconscious for success with the every-day positive thinking winners experience. Chances are they have plugged-up the creative genius of their subconscious with years of living with a negative mind set. There have been too many practices where they were looking for miscues; too many matches where their strategy was based on "mistake correction" or expecting the very worst outcome.

Sound familiar? Hopefully not too familiar! But if our description rings a bell and you are ready for a change, we have a simple cybernetic cure. It's called the **Cumulative Positive Mind Set.** Please understand that the instinct to make the right decisions at the right time will not develop overnight. It may take some time to unravel your negative web of thinking and tap the full instinctive power of your subconscious. However, the commitment to change can be achieved in an instant. Meaning, now! Are you with us?

HOW TO DEVELOP THE CUMULATIVE POSITIVE MIND SET

1. Develop a positive attitude whenever things go wrong by playing the **What's good about it?** game. By identifying ten reasons why what has happened is good you are immediately improving your state of mind. Always think **benefit** first no matter what happens.

2. Avoid thoughts or expressions of fear, frustration, or boredom before or after decision-making. They are negative mind-set traps that clog the creative juices that flow from your subconscious. When these "dream destroyers" appear, **act as if** you are courageous when feeling fearful, poised when feeling frustrated, and excited when feeling bored. With time your subconscious will cooperate.

3. Accept life's twists and turns. Resistance is another powerful negative mind-set trap. Learn to go with the flow for a change and see if you don't feel more energized and positive afterwards. For example, should an official make a bad call or a key player go down with an injury or sickness before a key match, stop complaining and accept it as an opportunity for individual and team growth.

4. Stop concerning yourself about the outcome of every decision you make! It's another negative mind-set trap and a terrible waste of energy as well. You must never think about a negative outcome either. You already know that thoughts repeated enough times become self-fulfilling prophecies.

5. Never feel sorry for yourself regardless of the outcome. Think: do life's breaks go to people who feel sorry for themselves? Want proof? The next time you feel sorry for yourself see how many correct decisions you make and how many favorable breaks you experience immediately afterwards.

6. Tell your subconsious what you want from it in specific terms. If you want to make correct decisions, tell it. **"I want the power to make correct decisions."** If it's an outcome you want, picture that outcome exactly the way you want it to happen. If the outcome doesn't work out, it's still all good. Remember:

Success comes from good judgment;
good judgment comes from experience;
experience comes from bad judgment.

As we said… it's all for the best.

Well Coach, do you want to catch a break and make the right calls on the sideline of a volleyball court (and in life)? Free your subconscious from the self-inflicted web of negative thinking and start developing a **Cumulative Positive Mind Set.** This means letting go of old strategies like griping, grumbling, complaining, pointing fingers, whining, and regretting. Are you prepared to say good-bye to these old friends and say hello to the **Cumulative Positive Mind Set?**

Just think of it this way: everytime you do something positive, a point is being put on a score-board. Score enough points and you will be enjoying some wonderful dividends. **A final thought before you go out to score those points: Can you grasp the concept of what you will become in the process of living a life rich with positive thinking and doing? Awesome concept.**

Chapter Thirteen

HOW TO BECOME A PRIME TIME PLAYER

"Should you need to doubt, doubt your doubts… never your quest."
San Giopani

Each competitive situation offers a creative opportunity for success. The so-called money player in sports is the athlete who is at his or her best under the stimulus of a challenge. John F. Kennedy once said, "There are no great men, only great opportunities."

Do you want to be a prime time money player? There is a price to pay and a progression to learn.

1. Learn playing skills under conditions where you will not be overmotivated. Overmotivation leads to overtrying which leads to incomplete plays. At the beginning, skills are best learned under conditions where there is little pressure. The more completions during the learning process the better. For example, try to develop your serving, blocking, and digging skills, playing at a three-quarter or #7 speed effort until there is a consistency of completions. Avoid overtrying at any cost. Act detached and stay detached. An overtrying effort interferes with thinking and doing. Your automatic success mechanism becomes jammed by too much effort. Have you noticed how many times your serve goes off target when an overtrying effort is involved? Control your speed effort, and success will become the name of your game.

2. The effort speeds apply to mental practice as well. At the start, the imagery should include no competitive or emotional details. Make your mental movies purely instructional. You are watching, not participating in the action.

3. Now run the action of your movies at a slow motion speed. Half or #5 speed is perfect. Enter the action. Let it become a first person, inside-out, action movie. Feel yourself finishing off the play exactly as planned.

4. In the final phase quicken the action and make your mental exercise an **everything on the line** game experience. Your mental practice must be as game-like and combative as you can make it. The opposition is aggressive. Your team is down a point. It's their serve! Unless your mental movie approximates the excitement and uncertainty of an actual match, prime time programming will not be effective. Do you hear the roar of the friendly crowd at the end of your impressive performance or the displeasure of the opponents' home crowd?

5. Learn to react to a crucial game situation with an aggressive "I can make a difference" attitude rather than a defensive, "I hope I don't make a mistake," mind-set. You must want to respond to a challenge, not hide from it. Keep your purpose in mind. Life is short! Your playing career is even shorter. The fear of making a mistake should not bother you. Realize that the worst outcome is not the mistake itself but the loss of an irretrievable opportunity by failing to seize the moment. The secret of the clutch performer lies in the attitude of aggressively accepting every crisis as a creative opportunity.

   The worst thing you can do is hope you don't "mess it up!" What you are really doing is adopting the same evasive attitude by which underachievers live their lives. Be fearless! Accept the challenge of the moment for what it is...a fleeting opportunity.

6. Learn to evaluate the so-called life and death situations in true perspective. Before it's too late you must understand what you do on the court today is only tomorrow's trivia, an event few remember or really care about. No game is composed of real life and death situations, just many small challenges. If you fail at one, learn from it and get ready for the next one. Prime time players do not live in the past or the future while competing... only the present. Be a **here and now athlete.** The philosophy that everything depends on one single play is pure nonsense! There are hundreds of plays in the match. What is the difference if you miss a serve in the first game or the last?

   Bob Dylan sings **"If you ain't got nothing, you've got nothing to lose."** Not a bad attitude to live or play by. If you think about it, how can you lose something you never had? That is not negative thinking. It's a great strategy for reducing anxiety and increasing your risk-taking ability.

7. Reframe that feeling you experience in your gut before and during a match as excitement, not fear or anxiety. Excitement is an empowering emotion that supports peak performance. All successful athletes experience the feeling of excitement in competition. When directed toward a positive goal picture, excitement generates additional strength, speed, and courage — the fight part of the fight-or-flight syndrome. A negative goal picture is nature's way of equipping you for escape and a losing effort. Remember the time Dave's team avoided a potentially bad experience by reframing the event of the opponents' pep

band playing during pre-match warm-up? He simply helped his team reframe how much fun it was warming up to the booming music.

8. Still tentative in prime time? Ask yourself this question: "What's the worst thing that can happen to me if I fail?" Imagine looking into your crystal ball. You are in the future, a short time after the end of the current season. See yourself looking back to the past season. Because you played it safe and never took chances, can you see the pile of lost opportunities you left behind? Since you didn't play as aggressively as you should have, what do you hear your teammates and your coach saying about you now? What do you think of yourself? Not a pleasant sight to remember.

Now try this one on for size. You just completed a season in which you stepped up in the clutch to take that last set and put it to the floor or made that last big defensive play that turned the momentum of the match around. More than several times you succeeded. Continue to look in the crystal ball and describe the image you see of yourself, now that you took aggressive action in a pivotal game. Do you see the inner strength, a vitality, an incredible look of determination and courage in your facial expression? What do you think your friends, teammates, coach, and parents are saying about your decisive performance now? Not a bad feeling...is it? So which series of images in the crystal ball do you prefer to see after the season is over? Do you really want to be a step-up performer or not? The choice is yours! There will be no doubting allowed!

Ready to move to the court? Turn the page and discover the on the court proof that **Volleyball Cybernetics** can put you in charge of your volleyball destiny.

PART FOUR
On The Court...

*"You cannot discover new oceans unless you have
the courage to lose sight of the shore."*
Andre Gide

Chapter Fourteen

THE PROOF... THE ACHIEVEMENT CARD

"People with goals succeed because they know where they're going."
Earl Nightingale

The proof in the pudding is in the **"seeing."** Athletes and coaches are no exception. They love to see results — especially those they can measure.

In order to prove to the camp athletes that **Cybernetics Training** works, we give the campers a 5 x 8 Achievement Card (see illustration on page 120) on the first day. They use the card to measure their skill level in several areas before and after they apply some of our inner game methods. The card lists nine different challenges including serving percentage, serving target accuracy, quickness, agility, setting, passing, and jumping ability.

For most of the tests there is either a 30-second time limit or a consecutive best factor, for example, the number of serves in a row. A score is then recorded on the card. The challenges include the following:

30 Second Challenges

Side Step
Forearm Passing: To Self

Challenges

Vertical Jump
Serving Percentage
Serving Target Zone Accuracy

Personal Best Challenges

Individual Consecutive: Passing, Setting, and Serving
Pair Consecutive: Passing, Setting

"Yes, I Can!"
Volleyball Camp Achievement Card

Name _____

School _____ Grade _____

Position played _____

	Pretest	1	2	3	4	Total+/-
SIDE STEP (30 Seconds)						
FOREARM PASSING TO SELF (30sec.)						
Vertical Pretest Jump Posttest Total inches +/-						
SERVING Zone _____ Zone _____ Zone _____						

TOTAL

PERSONAL BEST

	Individual Consecutive	Total of 5 best attempts
Serving		
Passing		
Setting		
	Pair Consecutive	Total of 5 best attempts
Passing		
Setting		

The first challenge is the **Side Step Quickness Challenge.** The procedure is to test each athlete's lateral foot quickness in 30 seconds and then record the results on the Achievement Card. After the athletes learn our **VAK Modeling Method,** they are immediately retested and scored.

SIDE STEP QUICKNESS CHALLENGE

Athletes pair off. One performs a side-step shuffle back and forth across a basketball 3 second lane as the partner scores the results. There is an imaginary line halfway between the two real lane lines. For each line the athlete side steps over or on she receives a point. The athlete's goal is to side step over as many lines as possible in 30 seconds. The player's partner counts the lines and then takes a turn.

Next, we introduce the **VAK Mind Training Method** as the campers model the quickest feet in the gym. Then the athlete, with no further practice, is retested with the score being recorded on the card. When the before and after scores are compared, the athlete realizes what the power of the mind can accomplish.

MODELING WITH VAK

After all the athletes are scored on the initial Side Step Test, we ask the two campers with the best scores to become the role models for the VAK. The role models proceed to side step again over the lines (the two real and one imaginary). The campers watch and do the following:

V for Visual: As the quickest feet in the gym perform, we tell them: "Imagine that your eyes are a video camera permanently recording the action of the quick feet by simply watching." We suggest that they focus on the quick feet as they glide across the lane and observe the quick change of direction. Then we say, "Close, open, and close your eyes until you can commit to memory those winning, quick feet moving back and forth with lightning speed."

A for Audio: After a brief rest the models side step again. The campers' focus is now audio. We tell them, "Listen carefully to the quick feet attacking the lines. With the rhythm of the moving steps say **'Quick! Quick! Quick!'** to yourself."

K for Kinesthetic: The volunteers rest for a few seconds before they side step one last time. We then say, "Imagine what it would feel like if you were inside those shoes on the quick feet. Mentally jump inside the winners' shoes. **Act as if** your feet are inside those incredibly quick shoes. Feel the amazing quickness."

MENTALLY SET A HIGHER SCORE BY TWO

Before being retested the campers are asked to:

1. Repeat **"Quick! Quick! Quick!"** for 30 seconds.
2. Establish a new goal for themselves and their subconscious.

A previous score of 48 mentally becomes a score of 50. All the campers are asked to look up at the gym's scoreboard and imagine their first score has already increased by two. We say, "See the higher score clearly in your mind's eye." By doing this they are telling their subconscious, "See this...do this!" This new 'higher by two' score is what I want you to achieve for me." As they perform the side steps they must recite the power words, **"Quick! Quick! Quick!"** at that faster cadence.

The outcome is astonishing. Most athletes reach the higher goal. It's not uncommon to see campers improve their scores by ten or more! Scores have, in fact, increased by over twenty lines!!

Why don't you try the **Side Step Challenge** with several friends. Follow the process exactly as we've recommended. Score each other and then **VAK** the quickest feet. Set a higher score by two and then retest. You'll have proof that this **VAK** stuff works, but what is more important, you'll have proof that you have an **Internal Success Mechanism** and you now know how to operate it. Check out the rest of the Achievement Card Challenges and have some fun.

FOREARM SELF PASSING CHALLENGE

You're on the court away from the net with a volleyball. You have 30 seconds to make as many good forearm passes to yourself as you can. Since the net is slightly higher than 7 feet 4 inches each pass must travel at least 10 feet high. Score the total amount of good passes you make in the time allowed. Remember, they do not have to be consecutive. Make sure to emphasize proper passing technique. This includes a sturdy base of support with one foot slightly in front and a proper passing platform with the base of the thumbs and forearms together forming an even surface. The wrists should be rotated downward toward the floor.

Now **VAK** the best. Model someone who is a skilled passer and has a top score.

V for Visual: Visually study the passer's form, the smooth control, and accuracy of the model's passes a dozen or more times.

A for Auditory: Repeat the words **"Smooth and Controlled."** After an accurate pass, add the anchor word **"Yes!"** This will help you lock in that good feeling of success.

K for Kinesthetic: Mentally jump inside the good passer and imagine what it would feel like to pass a ball with the same grace and efficiency as your role model. Try to **feel** the soft texture of the ball as it rebounds off your forearms. **Feel** the successful finish at least a dozen times and don't forget to say **Yes!** after each successful pass.

  Retest: Before you retest, repeat the power words **"Smooth and Controlled"... "Yes!"** for at least 30 seconds. Establish a higher score by imagining your previous best increasing by two passes on the gym's scoreboard. Then go for it as you recite the power words with each pass. Record, compare, and enjoy your improvement. Congratulations!

INDIVIDUAL CONSECUTIVE FOREARM PASSING CHALLENGE

This is similar to the forearm self passing challenge only there is no time limit. Without a time limit, count how many accurate passes you can make to yourself in a row. Once the ball hits the floor, or does not travel at least 10 feet high, or is hit illegally, the challenge ends. Your goal is to increase your personal best score. Remember to include the verbal commands with each pass.

INDIVIDUAL CONSECUTIVE SETS CHALLENGE

This is exactly the same as the **Consecutive Forearm Passing Challenge** except you will be testing your ability to set to yourself. Correct setting technique must be used.

  Setting Tips: Ball should be received in line with the forehead. Make sure to contact the ball only with the pads of the fingers and thumbs. Let the hands act as **springs** as they bend back toward the head upon contact with the ball and then **spring** forward upon release of the ball. Extend the arms completely upward during the follow-through.

Now, model the best in the gym.

V for Visual: Watch your team's best setter set the ball at least a dozen times. Pay special attention to her fluid, soft setting motion. Appreciate her balanced body positioning and complete follow through. Be especially aware of the accuracy of her sets.

A for Auditory: Listen to the **softness** of her sets. Memorize the sound of the ball contacting the pads of her fingers and thumbs. Notice how quiet the sound is. Start to say to yourself, **"Soft and Smooth"** as you observe the setting star smoothly and with complete control set the ball accurately to her target over and over again. Recite to yourself with each set the power words: **"Soft and Smooth."**

K for Kinesthetic: Ready to mentally jump inside the setter's body and go for the winner's ride? Can you feel the winner's confidence, control, and mastery? Sure you can!

　　Retest: Practice your **"Soft and Smooth"** verbal commands for 30 seconds. Before retesting, set a goal two points higher than your previous score. If your first score was **32**, go for **34**. Imagine **34** lighting up on the scoreboard as if your achievement has just happened. Again remember to recite the command words with each set. Compare the two scores and enjoy the feeling of accomplishment.

CONSECUTIVE PASSING AND SETTING CHALLENGES:
WITH A PARTNER

The rules are identical to the **Individual Consecutive Passing** and **Setting Challenges** only now you are working with a partner. The **VAK** process still holds.

SERVING PERCENTAGE CHALLENGE

You will use **The Ultimate Serving Method** as it is explained in Chapter Sixteen. Before you learn **The Method,** you will attempt 10 serves and record the number of successes. After you learn **The Method,** retest your serving accuracy by taking 10 more serves.

SERVING ZONE ACCURACY CHALLENGE

Again you'll test your accuracy before learning **The Ultimate Serving Method.** Serve 10 balls to each of the three zones across the opponents' back row (see serving chart on page 131). Record the number of successful serves to each zone. After you learn **The Method** strive to improve your best out of 10 score.

There is no doubt in our minds that **VAK Technology** can improve your game. After you experience the increased foot quickness in the **Side Step Challenge,** there should be no doubt in your mind either. Use **VAK** to change any part of your game. Just keep this in mind: Wherever there is a winner, there is a role model for you to follow. **So VAK away!**

Now if you're ready to dramatically improve your vertical jumping ability, turn the page and discover how to take your "vertical" to the limit… and beyond.

Chapter Fifteen

HOW TO IMPROVE YOUR VERTICAL JUMPING ABILITY

"They can because they think they can."

Virgil

Time to walk our talk and test the power of your subconscious with our **VAK** formula, and one of the most anticipated events at camp — the **Vertical Jump Challenge.**

Stan remembers the first time he reprogrammed an athlete to jump higher. The year was 1976 and the basketball camp was at Eckard College in St. Petersburg, Florida. The event was so spectacular that the ***St. Petersburg Evening Independent*** featured it in their evening edition.

"Close your eyes," the youngster was told. "Relax by using the breathing exercise that we talked about. Now, picture yourself clearly touching the rim. After you've formed this picture vividly in your mind and you feel ready, go ahead and do it. Get the rim!"

The player stood there and thought for endless seconds. Slowly he ran to the basket and jumped. Not only did he touch the rim for the first time in his life, he had an inch or two to spare. The six-footer had never come closer than three or four inches. Jim Harley, camp director, called the demonstration 'amazing.' Some campers nearly fell to the floor. Their eyeballs were as big as saucers. There was no magic, no mirrors, no tricks. It was just one example of mind control, the results of a forty-five minute lecture on Cybernetics Training by Stan Kellner.*

---

* As it appeared in the *St. Petersburg Evening Independent,* Florida, June 1976.

By now you should know how and why this athlete suddenly found the hidden capacity to explode and improve his vertical jump beyond the highest level it had ever been. Most athletes have the potential for jumping higher. The only requirements for improving your vertical jump are that you must want to jump higher, and not be afraid to fail. If you have never reached the basketball rim, here's the alternate plan we use at our **"Yes, I Can!" Volleyball Camp:**

You can use a vertical jump chart that is attached to the wall. Take one step and jump at the chart until you feel confident that you've achieved your best jump (best score) to the inch. If no jump chart is available and your best jump is several inches short of the basketball rim, the bottom of the backboard, or the bottom of the net, each object also presents an excellent target to go for. The jumping process includes these five steps:

1. **Mentally picture your new vertical jumping target.**
2. **Quiet your mind and body.**
3. **Use the power of visualization to mentally lower your jumping target.**
4. **Create a power state of mind by centering all of your mental powers on a successful end-result picture.**
5. **Stay with the jumping until you achieve your new goal.**

If you are jumping at a jump chart positioned against the wall, use a one or two step approach. If the rim, backboard, or net is your target then a running start of three to five steps at an angle of your choice is allowed.

Now do this:

1. Stand one step off to the side of the vertical jump chart. Add two inches to your best jump (best height) and focus your full attention on that two inch higher spot on the chart. Memorize each and every detail of that higher mark on the chart, for example, the width of the tape and the color and shape of the numbers. Close your eyes and vividly imagine your hand touching your goal on the chart. If you have trouble **seeing** the marker with your eyes closed, open and close your eyes until you can imagine the marker with your eyes closed.

2. With your eyes closed quiet your mind and body by paying close attention to your breathing rhythm. On each exhalation, as you feel the air escaping through your nose and mouth, say to yourself **"Let Go."** Feel the tension flowing out. Feel the pressure of the moment flowing out of your body. You are feeling very relaxed and comfortable. Imagine all the limiting beliefs of how high you can jump flow out with each breath. You should feel very comfortable.

3. Now begin to pay attention to each inward breath passing through your nose and mouth. As the air fills your lungs feel yourself becoming lighter and stronger. Imagine there is a magic mixture in the air you're breathing making you actually feel lighter and stronger. A sensational source of power is filling your lungs. On each inhalation say, **"Light and Strong."** Sense the large muscles of your legs absorbing the energy flow from the air you're

inhaling. Can you feel your body becoming lighter and stronger with each inhalation as you repeat, **"Light and Strong"**?

Now imagine a large funnel above your head. Visualize a powerful column of bright, white energy coming from high above you flowing through this funnel and into the top of your head. Feel this column of cosmic energy pouring through your head, down your neck, and into your chest cavity charging your body with incredible energy. Feel your legs become more powerful and energized like two powerful springs. Each muscle fiber, each cell, each molecule, each atom in the muscles of your legs is becoming electrically charged by the white energy flowing through your body. Can you feel how strong, energized, and light you are?

4. Remember, your mind can create any image you want. With your eyes still closed return to the mental image of the marker and mentally lower the entire chart two inches. Create an image of your fingers touching the spot on the chart you desire to achieve. At first make it a still picture. Hold the image several seconds in your mind until it becomes so big and clear that you can actually feel the texture of the chart's surface on your hand.

Now imagine watching yourself confidently stepping, gathering, and exploding upwards as you touch your new goal. See yourself reaching your goal several times. Now make it a first-person experience. Travel inside the movie and feel yourself stepping up, jumping, and touching that target on the chart. You're locked into a **Power State** of mind, so keep jumping until you achieve your goal.

THE POWER OF CHANGING BODY LANGUAGE WITH MODELING

Occasionally when an athlete has not achieved his or her jumping goal, Stan quickly empowers the frustrated athlete by changing the athlete's body language. He asks the jumper to stand directly in front of him and play a game called **Follow the Leader.** Stan gets into a **Power State** himself by thinking how great it would feel if he jumped higher than he had ever jumped before. **"Mirror me!"** Stan tells the athlete. "I want you to copy everything that you see from the way that I'm standing, holding my shoulders back, breathing deeply, my facial expressions, and the intense look in my eyes. Whatever you see copy exactly." After about thirty seconds of some nonverbal modeling Stan tells the athlete, "You now have the power! Go ahead and do it!" When the athlete suddenly reaches his or her goal, the doubters in the gym become believers.

What's Next On Your Success Agenda?

The jumping event is not supernatural or mysterious. It is natural and scientific. You have simply reprogrammed a new belief into your automatic **Internal Success System.** The belief supplied the "know-how." So what's next on your wish list? What is it that you really want? Which skills and attitudes will best help you live your dream:

1. More intensity on defense
2. Improved serving percentage and accuracy
3. Increased hitting percentage and power
4. Stepping up as a prime time performer
5. Freedom to make mistakes
6. Winning attitudes such as courage, aggressiveness, second effort, poise, and self-confidence
7. More fun playing volleyball

With the **FAST** and **VAK** formulas of success in your hands and the **Internal Success System** in your head, it's time to move to the serving end of the court and discover the **Ultimate Serving Method.**

Chapter Sixteen

THE ULTIMATE SERVING METHOD
OR HOW TO BECOME AN AWESOME SERVING MACHINE

"Inside of every server there is a great server waiting to get out."
Stan Kellner

Does a funny thing happen to your serve on the way to match point? Does the ball wind up in the net or out of bounds? Maybe it is time to look in a new direction to solve your inconsistent serve...inwardly, and discover the magic of **The Ultimate Serving Method.**

THE PERSONAL BEST GAME

Before we introduce you to our "inside-out" serving method, let's test your current serving accuracy with a game called **Personal Best.** It's important to know exactly how good your serve is so that after you learn **The Method** you can measure your improvement.

The object of the Personal Best Game is to determine how many consecutive serves you can make within 5 minutes. If you're a plus 95% server already, your personal best challenge will be to see how many consecutive serves you can hit to a specific target area on the court within 5 minutes. See Diagram below.

Rules: Once you miss, begin a new count. You need not rush your serve. Make as many serves in a row as possible and remember the total of your best string.

SERVING ZONES DIAGRAM

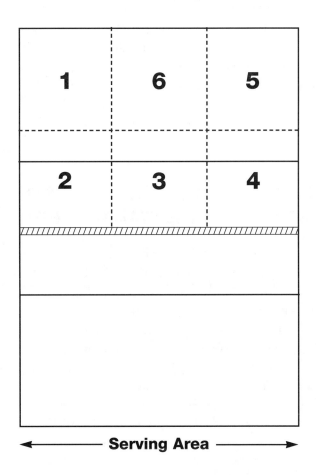

← **Serving Area** →

THE METHOD'S SECRETS

The road **The Method** takes leads directly to the control center for your performance, your mind. The analogy of the human brain and the electronic computer is well established. **The Method** will show you how to successfully train your biological computer for a stronger and more accurate serve. The key to the success of **The Method** will be to learn how to operate the internal mechanism that produces all of your habits of thinking and doing... the subconscious. This is the same internal mechanism that automatically controls the flight and finish of your serve.

The Ultimate Serving Method works because:

1. You will make direct contact with your subconscious telling it what you want, rather than it telling you what it wants you to do! By providing your computer-like subconscious with the thinking of the winner, you will soon have a more reliable serve.

2. Remember your subconscious cannot tell the difference between a real and a vividly imagined experience. This incredible fact creates all kinds of opportunities for retraining your subconscious with the help of positive visualization and self-talk statements.

3. You will learn how to fully utilize the verbal ability of the left side of your brain (the "thinking" side) and the visual ability of the right side (the "just do it" side) in a harmonious effort. Too often it's the judgmental left side of the brain that interferes with the action of your serve by providing your subconscious with the wrong kind of feedback instructions. You already know what too much thinking or the wrong kind of thinking can do to your serve. It's like putting the wrong software into an electronic computer and expecting the correct answers. Guess again.

ANCHORING THREE INNER ESSENTIALS INTO YOUR MENTAL COMPUTER

Anchoring is the technique of setting up a physical routine to trigger a specific response. Most players already have a serving routine — bouncing the ball a certain number of times, standing or holding the ball a certain way, etc. Here is our inner-game routine (anchor) that can help you lock into an incredible serving groove.

There are three inner essentials that need to be learned in order for you to master the serve. They are the focus, feel, and finish of your serve. Your intention will be to anchor three individual command words by saying these words aloud (or to yourself) as you simultaneously perform the physical actions of the serve. The words you will say are:

1. **SIGHT!** as you focus your full attention on the toss of the ball to begin your serve.
2. **FEEL!** as you begin to swing your arm forward, make contact with the ball and observe its perfect flight over the net.
3. **YES!** as you observe the ball reach its intended target.

LEARNING HOW TO SUCCESSFULLY MISS A SERVE

With or without **The Method,** your serve will not always be on target. When this happens you must learn how to clear away any feelings of doubt and frustration that may lead to an **overtrying** effort on your next serve. A clear and uncluttered state of mind is essential for the server to acquire a consistently confident serving groove. This is accomplished by simply saying the word: **CLEAR!...(instead of the word YES!) after an errant serve.** As you already know, **CLEAR!** helps erase those negative emotions that linger around after playing mistakes and create havoc with your subconscious.

Again develop a feeling of **CLEAR!** by focusing your eyes on any white and uncluttered surface (wall or sheet of paper). Continue to open and close your eyes, each time saying **CLEAR!** to yourself, until you can visualize the clear surface with your eyes closed. Remember, in competition **CLEAR!** is recited with either open or closed eyes.

THE ADVANTAGES OF LINKING WORDS TO THE SERVING ACTION:

1. **Eliminates the possibility of negative thinking:** Since two thoughts cannot occupy your mind at the same time, reciting the words **SIGHT! FEEL! YES!** in a smooth cadence locks out all negative thinking.

2. **Sharpens concentration:** By associating key words to key actions, your right and left brain are forced to center their undivided attention together on the task at hand.

3. **Locks you into a fantastic serving groove:** When speaking these power words in a smooth, confident rhythm, you will discover your serve is equally smooth, confident, and unrushed. Remember these words are timed and associated with successful actions and are stored together as one unit. Say the words and you naturally experience the winning feeling to which they have been linked.

4. **Provides programming command words that can be used away from the court:** Each time you recite the words **SIGHT! FEEL! YES!** along with visualizing a successful serve, you will be supplying your subconscious with signals of success. One hundred repetitions of **SIGHT! FEEL! YES!** while simultaneously visualizing a winning serve means 100 successful serving experiences to your impressionable subconscious.

5. **Provides a powerful pre-serve routine:** By repeating the command word **YES!** before you serve, you will automatically recapture that feeling of success that has been associated with it.

THE METHOD

STEP 1: HOW TO DEVELOP THE POWER OF FOCUS

Focus is important because it allows you to stay with what you want to do rather than what you don't want to do! The initial step of **The Method** is the sighting of your first target, the ball. Staying in the **here and now** as you serve is essential. This means **not** remembering your last missed serve, worrying about the direction of your current serve, thinking about the importance of the serve, or allowing the deadly silence while everyone in the gym awaits your serve to bother you.

Standing at the 10 foot (3 meter) line, toss the ball above your head. Say the command word SIGHT! as you focus your eyes on the ball. Do this 10 times without serving the ball. Allow the ball to drop to the floor. Then serve 10 times saying SIGHT! as you toss the ball. Allow the ball to go wherever it wants after contact is made. Successful serves are not important at this time. Linking the word SIGHT! with eye contact on the toss is essential.

Skill Tip: Be certain that your toss is landing directly in line and slightly in front of your right foot (right handed server).

STEP 2: HOW TO DEVELOP THE CONFIDENT FEELING

What is it that you want to feel while serving? No, it's not the feel of leather as you make your toss and contact the ball. We're talking about that inner sense of confidence. It is the positive expectation that the ball will travel straight and true over the net to its intended destination. It is that mental picture of success and the associated feeling of confidence that you want to develop.

The feeling of success acts as a homing device, guiding the flight and finish of your serve. By linking the sight of a successful serve with the word **FEEL!**, you are storing in your mental computer this all important confident feeling along with the word. Say the word and you recapture the feeling of success to which it has been anchored (linked).

Standing at the same 10 foot line begin to easily serve the ball over the net and into the opponent's court:

1. On the toss of the ball above your head say the word **SIGHT!**
2. Then as you begin your armswing forward say the command word **FEEL!** Continue to say FEEL! as long as you can into the ball's flight over the net (**FEEEEEEL!**).

Note: Make sure that FEEL! is spoken in a confident tone. Also stretch the FEEL! command word throughout most of the ball's flight by adding as many E's as needed.

STEP 3: COMBINING SIGHT - FEEL! TOGETHER ON THE SERVE

Still serving from the 10 foot line, the next step will be to eliminate any time gap between **SIGHT!** and **FEEL!** Attach the words **SIGHT!** and **FEEL!** together in a continuous rhythm with the toss and the serving action. Continue to serve from the 10 foot line for several minutes, saying the word **SIGHT!** on the toss and immediately adding the word **FEEL!** as soon as you begin your armswing. Think of **SIGHT-FEEL!** as a (two syllable) one word command with no pause between the two words. No time to think, either.

Continue to serve from this shortened service line until the reciting of **SIGHT-FEEL!** with the serve is automatic.

> *Skill Tip: Remember, if you're a right handed server, your left foot is slightly ahead of the right foot in a stance slightly wider than the width of your shoulders. Say SIGHT! as you begin to step with your left foot and toss the ball and then FEEL! as you begin your armswing.*

STEP 4: HOW TO LOCK IN THAT CONFIDENT FEELING SERVE AFTER SERVE

Now you are ready to push one more key on your mental keyboard. Add the final word **YES!** or **CLEAR!** to the **SIGHT-FEEL!** verbal sequence. You want to be able to lock in that **"I can't miss"** feeling the 95% servers enjoy and lock out that **"I can't"** feeling the inconsistent server experiences.

Still serving from the 10 foot line, simply add the anchor word **YES!** to a successful serve (**SIGHT-FEEL-YES!**) or **CLEAR!** to an unsuccessful serve (**SIGHT-FEEL-CLEAR!**).

The importance of clearing your mental computer of all negative emotions cannot be underestimated. Fear and frustration can lead you to an overtrying effort on your next serve. You can practice serving from dawn to dusk, but unless you learn how to detach yourself from the emotional debris of a serving mistake, you'll always be remembered as that streaky, inconsistent server who folded in prime time. So make it your habit to **CLEAR!** after each miss while serving during drills and then observe what happens to your serving consistency.

ADD YOUR FAVORITE PHYSICAL ANCHOR AFTER A SUCCESS

As you say the verbal anchor (**YES!**) for a good serve, add a physical anchor to further lock in that winning feeling. Clenching a fist or snapping the fingers of one hand will do. Our favorite physical anchor for **CLEAR!** is making the baseball umpire's safe sign with both hands (palms down) while looking up toward the heavens.

THE IMPORTANCE OF A PRE-SERVE VERBAL ROUTINE

Here is our recommended pre-serve routine. Just before serving do this:

- Pick a spot in the opponents' court where you want the ball to go. Now confidently say the word **YES!** to yourself as you visualize your serve landing at the spot of your choice.

- If it is your habit to bounce the ball before serving, keep your mind busy by saying the word **BOUNCE!** during each bounce. This keeps your mind free of any interfering thoughts.

- It will help if you visualize the ball's flight as a trail of lighted balls traveling its chosen path. It's not how long you hold this image, but how well. In time you'll be surprised how quickly and vividly you're able to visualize the desired flight and finish of your serve.

- Now employ the three words as you serve:

> **SIGHT! FEEL! ... YES!**   with the good serve
>
> **SIGHT! FEEL! ... CLEAR!**   with the misplaced serve

Inner Skill Tip: While serving make sure you adopt the attitude of **let it happen** rather than **make it happen.** Trying too hard to make it happen causes your muscles to tighten up. **Let it happen** tells your subconscious that you trust it to get the job done. In the search for success in anything, **trust is a must!** We tell athletes at camp if they are having a problem trusting their serve then simply **"act as if"** you trust it. In time your subconscious will not know the difference.

WORKING YOUR WAY BACK TO THE ENDLINE

Stay at the 10 foot line until you make three consecutive serves using both the pre-serve routine (**YES!**) and the command words (**SIGHT! FEEL! YES!**). Then take two steps back and continue using **The Method** until you make three more in a row. Continue serving, backing up two more steps (after each set of three consecutive good serves), until you reach the endline.

Note: If you reach a distance at which you are unable to make three consecutive serves, this is where you should stay until you improve your consistency and reach the consecutive serve goal. At the **"Yes, I Can!" Camp** there is no serving line during matches. It is important that you experience success using **The Method** regardless of the distance from the net. Confidence multiplies when positive results occur. If you have trouble serving consistently from the endline, you will be amazed how quickly you develop a strong regulation serve once you learn **The Method** closer to the net.

THE NEXT LEVEL

After mastering the **Ultimate Serving Method,** take your serving accuracy to the next level by using **The Method** to improve your aggressive ace serve to a specific zone. How? Simply add the number of the serving zone (at which you are serving for the ace) to the pre-serve verbal routine **YES!** and replace the word **FEEL!** with that same number during the serve verbal routine.

For example: Say your goal is to aggressively serve for an ace to zone 5 — instead of just safely serving to zone 5. Your entire routine would now be to aggressively say **5! YES!** to yourself before serving and then say <u>**SIGHT! 5! YES!**</u> while you serve. Using the number of the serving zone instead of the word **FEEL!**, allows you to lock into a specific target area with a more aggressive, confident feeling when going for an ace.

DEVELOPING DETACHMENT WITH AN AFFIRMATION

Would you like to become an awesome serving machine, someone who can perform emotionally detached from the importance of the moment? Why not tell your reliable habitmaker, the subconscious, that you want to become a super cool serving machine capable of serving one winner after another? Your impressionable subconscious will listen. When you tell it what you want, make sure to say it in a tone of voice that is convincing. Tell your subconscious this:

> ## "I AM A SERVING MACHINE!"

This is not silliness. This affirmation, repeated to yourself in the most machine-like monotone will help you develop the poise and emotional detachment of a clutch server. Make it a habit to recite this affirmation to yourself before and after serves, or even off the court whenever possible. Before falling asleep at night or upon awakening are excellent times to communicate instructions to your subconscious. Then observe your cool emotional response after a miss and the increased consistency of your serve. Both will be better controlled in battle. Are 100 affirmations a day too high a price tag for a cool head and a more consistent serve?

We're not finished with the personal inner-game challenges. We also want you to recite to yourself 100 times each day the command **SIGHT! FEEL! ... YES!** along with a visualization of the perfect serve. Make it a first person mental movie and don't forget to add all the details of a prime time situation. You are not watching yourself serve, you are serving, and for a very important point.

THE FINAL TEST: EMPLOY THE METHOD WITH THE PERSONAL BEST GAME

Now, let's see how many consecutive serves you can attain using **The Method.** From the endline, return to the **Personal Best Game** for five minutes. Remember to employ both the **YES!** pre-serve routine and the **SIGHT! FEEL! YES!** commands with each serve.

Normally about 9 out of 10 servers improve significantly throughout the week of camp. But what happens to the servers who experience little or no improvement? What's their problem? It could be:

1. They still tend to take their misses too seriously. Our feeling: **They're not frustrated because they miss a serve...they miss a serve because they're easily frustrated!** Some are perfectionists. For them, any degree of frustration interferes with the winning feeling they should be looking to develop. Once they learn to clear away the backwash of a missed serve and develop a state of mind called **detachment,** they're surprised how many fewer serving mistakes they experience.

137

2. They continue to miss serves because their visual target is too vague. Getting the ball over the net is not exact enough. A more specific objective is needed. Define specifically where or whom you want as a target. Your subconscious works best on goals that are clearly defined.

A FINAL WORD

Expect to be challenged by an occasional serving dry spell. All challenges are good because they test your level of commitment and ability to handle frustration. Think of your mistakes as opportunities to develop the self-control needed to be a consistent winner. Should you hear yourself grumbling, "This mental stuff isn't working!" or "It's not my night!" immediately insert a new floppy disk into your mental computer. Empower yourself by repeating the affirmation **"I AM A SERVING MACHINE!"** and then serve. You'll enjoy the results.

Chapter Seventeen

TEAM SYNERGY

"The whole is greater than the sum of its parts."
Webster's Dictionary

Offense wins matches. Players know that. Defense wins championships. Coaches know that! Regardless of your opinion, bet the ranch on this, **TEAMWORK IS THE NAME OF THE GAME!**

Analyze any successful high school team, club, or college program and you'll find a commitment to teamwork. If teamwork is the name of the game the question is this: how can a coach increase the effectiveness of the team so that the whole is greater than the sum of its parts? In **Volleyball Cybernetics** the process is called **Team Synergy.** Second to none, **Synergy** offers a more direct route to team success than any other cybernetics method in this book.

The following information on **Team Synergy** is directed more to the coach reading this book than the athlete. Since it requires team participation and commitment, share **Synergy** with your coach and ask your coach to test its effectiveness in the gym during practice. We've seen what **Synergy** has done to increase the intensity of our camp games as a result of the extraordinary motivational powers it generates.

HOW DOES SYNERGY WORK?

Synergy multiplies the energy production of everyone on your team and produces a sustained sense of team purpose and unity throughout the team. There is a contagious element to **Synergy.** From the most motivated there is an enthusiasm and energy link that spreads like wild fire into the bodies of the least motivated.

SYNERGY: THE TEAM PLAN

In those special moments of a match when every player on the team is enthused, energized, focused, and 100% committed to playing together, the team is in a state of **Synergized Power. The definition of Synergy is the act of combining the energy of two or more people in a joint action.** When this occurs a multiplying energy effect is produced. Synergy is the process of pooling together the abilities and strengths of six players for a common purpose — to win a rally, for example. When a team is synergized everybody is focused and energized. No easy-to-hit holes are left open in the defense. The block is always up and in position. The opposition is forced to work exceptionally hard for points. Every offensive opportunity is used to mount an effective attack. Every serve is tough.

BUILDING TEAM SYNERGY

When six players go out on the court they bring with them six different levels of enthusiasm, energy, talent, and endurance. During the course of the game these factors fluctuate depending on a large number of physical and emotional elements. Any distraction for a single player can become an irreparable crack in the team's cohesiveness. Reasons for a decreased effort can range from a mistake, fatigue or a bad night's sleep to an official's poor call. Distractions can cause an otherwise hustling player to suddenly lose his or her focus on playing well. Interest is quickly lost in reading the opponent's movement or getting in the best position for a set or going to the floor to dig the ball.

But what about the tough teams that somehow manage to stay focused and energized regardless of the adversity? What's their secret? The answer is discipline, top physical conditioning, and a desire based on an unwavering sense of purpose. If you are not a **get in their face coach** the obvious question is, "How can the necessary discipline, conditioning, and a sustained sense of purpose be achieved?" The answer is **Team Synergy.**

A TEAM IS AS STRONG AS ITS WEAKEST PLAYER

When five players are playing physically tough, aggressive, smart, and inspired volleyball — dominating the net, keeping every ball off the floor, effectively attacking the opposition's defense, and one player isn't for whatever reason, the ball invariably finds the uninspired, brooding player and the team loses its efficiency. When a point or serve is lost in the process, there is a 100% decrease in efficiency. If you believe a team is as strong as its weakest player, as we do, then it's time to motivate the unmotivated, commit the uncommitted, and energize the unenergized.

THE FIRST STEP: ESTABLISH A SET OF TEAM RULES

Before you can incorporate **Synergy** into your practice and enjoy its bonding benefits, you need to clearly establish your team's on-the-court rules. Here are ours:

```
   1.  Get it!
   2.  Pass it!
   3.  Set it!
   4.  "Crush" it!
```

1. For a defensive player "**Get it!**" starts with reading the opponents' attack, moving decisively to cover the most probable attack angles, then getting to the ball if it comes his/her way.

2. "**Pass it!**" means putting the pass to the target, making it easier for the setter to use any of the offensive options available.

3. "**Set it!**" means overhand passing the ball into a position so that the ball can be successfully attacked by a teammate.

4. "**Crush it!**" is the act of putting the ball to the floor with a powerful, unreturnable spike.

THE SILVER BULLET:

Turning a "**Me-Too**" into a "**We-Too**" effort can be achieved by drawing on the entire team's energy force. All the effort comes from the players. Little emotional energy is required from the coach. No shouting and prodding from the coach is necessary, leading to less work for the coach and more fun for the players. Another advantage is the coach does not have to introduce a single new drill other than our **Team Synergy** to get results. Everything stays the same except for the improved outcome.

Coach: This is how to introduce **Synergy**:

1. Divide your squad into teams of four players.

2. Each four-player team joins hands to form a circle. Taking a strong, wide defensive stance, they shout in unison the first rule of **Team Synergy** three times, "**Get it! Get it! Get it!**" They should know that the louder they yell and the more emotion they put into it, the more committed they will become as a team.

3. In concert Rules #2, #3, and #4 are loudly chanted (three times).

4. The four-player teams then compete against one another in a shouting contest.

The cumulative effect is that as they scream away, other things happen. Body language, facial expressions, and an incredibly powerful state of mind develop. The act of joining hands allows each player to feel the intensity of the group's emotions. Ask the players not to hold hands as they chant a **Synergy Rule** and they will immediately feel the difference. The screaming of the rules becomes even more fun as the teams compete for some prize, anything from a water break to recognizing a successful effort with the entire team's applause. The meek and the shy are quickly exposed but they usually get plugged into the group's enthusiasm before long. They soon realize that the embarrassment of joining hands and screaming is a distant second to being part of an uninspired and losing team!

Just in case, Coach, some of your players think they are too "cool" to join hands, tell them to check out any pro football game on television. They'll see mammoth NFL athletes joining hands in the defensive huddles without embarrassment. Certainly your players can join hands in the privacy of their own gym.

SYNERGIZE YOUR DRILLS

Coach: You can reinforce all offensive and defensive skills and attitudes by forming **Synergy Circles** before and after a drill. For example, on the passing drills, the players join hands and shout, **"Pass it! Pass it! Pass it!"** Circles can be in groups of four, five, six, or the entire team. A team can synergize before the match in the locker room or on the court between games. Everybody joins hands in one big cooperative circle and chants a point of emphasis, **"Hit the Corners!"** or **"Set the Block!"** or **"Own the Net!"** For emphasis make certain the players shout the command three times.

QUEEN OF THE COURT

Queen of the Court is our special game that uses **Synergy** as its base of operation. It not only teaches the rules of team play, but it is as fun to play as it is exciting to watch. Here's how it's played:

1. **"Queen"** is either a three-on-three or four-on-four game with a third team involved.
2. The third team is beyond the endline (out of bounds) at the challenger's end of the court waiting its turn to enter the game. While they wait they circle-up and chant a **Team Synergy** rule three times loud and clear.
3. The challengers serve with rally scoring rules in effect. Either the serving or receiving team can score the point.
4. The action never stops. When a team wins a play, they go to the **Queen's** side of the court or stay put if they are already there, circle-up, and chant a **Team Synergy** rule three times loud and clear.
5. The team that loses the play retrieves the ball and goes to the end of the line on the "challenger's side."
6. There they join hands, circle-up, and synergize by shouting one of the four rules of **Synergy** three times.
7. The next team that was waiting its turn immediately steps on the challenger's side and serves.
8. If playing four-on-four teams must organize themselves in a diamond formation. There is one blocker, one setter to the right side and behind the 10 foot line, one directly across from the setter on the left side and one back row player at the center back position on the endline in the middle of the court. If playing three-on-three, teams can line up one of two ways:

a. *Players line up in a triangle formation with one player at the net at center front, while the remaining two players are about ten feet behind the ten foot line and ten feet in from the closest sideline. The player at the net acts as the setter.*

b. *All three players line up in back row positions, with one player lining up as a setter on the right sideline just behind the ten foot line. The other two players line up three feet above the endline and five feet in from the sideline to receive serve. Once the play begins, they slide to the basic LB and CB positions of a 6-back (centerback) defense. In this version, no blocking is allowed.*

9. After synergizing, the circle opens up, forming a straight line with the players' hands still joined (except for the outside hands of the end athletes), facing the court waiting its turn.

10. Each team keeps track of how many plays they win. The team with the most points at the end of a pre-set time limit wins the game.

MORE CHALLENGES

To make **"Queen"** even more challenging, add the following rules:

Tip Rule: All tip shots must travel at least to the 10 foot line. If a tip falls to the floor short of the line, the team that tipped the ball loses the play.

Overpass Rule: When the team receiving the serve overpasses the serve (sends it over the net), they automatically lose the play.

Coach, once you decide to commit to synergizing and playing **Queen of the Court** on a daily basis, you won't believe the carryover benefit in matches. Observe if your team challenges the ball at the net better, dives for balls near the floor better, attacks more aggressively, and plays tougher with more endurance. You'll see with your own eyes that **Team Synergy** works!

SYNERGY: THE WRITTEN PLAN

Write it down! The use of goal cards is an excellent method for fixing team goals more permanently.

1. **Establish a clear cut set of team goals.** Coach, a few days before a match write the word **SYNERGY** on a chalkboard. Discuss what your team must do in the next match to be successful. Discuss the opponents' offensive tendencies, including who their big hitters are. Clearly define what must be done defensively. Discuss your offensive goals. Where are their weaknesses? How can we take advantage of these weaknesses? Now under the word **SYNERGY** list your team goals for the match.

For example:

A. Establish a team serving percentage for success. 95% will do it.

B. Be aggressive at the net.

C. Serve receive: 80% team success.

D. Take away all line shots.

E. Attack the corners from the middle.

Make sure that you keep everything on the board in view of the players before and after the match as a reminder of your team's commitment to team effort. After the match, involve the players in the evaluation by asking with a show of hands whether each strategy was attained.

2. **Make a contract.** A couple of days before the match each player writes across the top of a 3x5 goal card (using a bold magic marker) the four **Team Synergy Rules: "Get it!" "Pass it!" "Set it!" "Crush it!"** Then they rewrite the same specific team goals listed on the chalkboard. In order to make the contract more meaningful, each player must sign the goal card, date it, and carry the goal card around with her until match time. Signing the goal card does not guarantee commitment, but it's a good beginning.

3. **Mentally program the goals.** Ask your players to find time at home to mentally visualize themselves making the plays necessary for team goal achievement. The two-step visualization process includes seeing (outside in) and feeling (inside out) themselves serving tough, winning the battle at the net, reading the opponents' attack, and digging their best shot.

There is an additional benefit of goal cards. Even if your team loses, setting specific strategy objectives allows players to achieve partial victories. After a loss it's important to feel that the match was not a total defeat. Team goal setting allows the players on the losing team to focus on what they did right in the match, not what they did wrong. With enough small victories, in time they'll be earning the big ones.

GOAL CARDS FOR INDIVIDUAL DEVELOPMENT

After the match goal cards can help a player concentrate on turning a playing weakness exposed during the match into a stronger skill. For instance, if the player was not getting off the net far enough for her attack approach, the player writes the cure on a goal card:

"GET OFF!"

The prescription must be positive and short. Two to four words are more than enough. Words like **"don't"** and **"avoid"** are words to be **"avoided"** at all costs. The goal card is placed where the player can easily see it as a constant reminder for the mental rehearsal. Remember to sign and date the card.

A SYNERGY DEMONSTRATION PROVES A POINT

Mike Gibson, our program director at camp, introduces **Team Synergy** to the campers with this simple but dramatic demonstration. A volunteer is brought up in front of the entire camp. Mike places a large plastic garbage can upside down on the gym floor in front of the camper. The camper is handed a baseball bat and told to hit the top of the garbage can with the bat as many times as he can in 30 seconds with the campers looking on silently. A second camper counts the hits. Mike then explains to the group the power of **Team Synergy** and its concept of **one for all and all for one.**

Next, the campers are told to offer the volunteer as much verbal support as possible by shouting encouragement. The volunteer is then given another 30 seconds to bang away at the garbage can, but this time with the entire group cheering the volunteer on with incredible emotion. The number of hits is once again counted. With the added encouragement, the volunteer always beats the first score. The entire camp realizes the **synergistic power** that exists when everybody pulls together for a common purpose.

TEAM SYNERGY LENDS A HELPING HAND

A camp coach related how a synergistic event helped his team to an amazing come from behind victory against a perennial power. Jeff Hicks's Medina Bees had just lost game one of their match with conference heavyweight Brecksville, 0-15. Between games Coach Hicks decided to change offenses, going from a 6-2 to a 5-1, even though he was playing an inexperienced sophomore setter who had never even seen a 5-1 before! Jeff quickly pulled his setter, Caroline, aside and explained the strategy change. Caroline's immediate reaction was first one of disbelief and then panic. Seeing this, Jeff stressed to his young setter that she was very capable of doing the job and that it wasn't that much different than playing in a 6-2. He quickly explained the obvious differences between the two offenses to Caroline, all the time emphasizing his confidence in her ability to do the job well. As the team headed back out on the floor for the start of game two, Coach Hicks reminded his captains to make sure everyone stayed positive no matter what was happening. After Caroline made an error on an early play, the entire team ran over to her and told her to forget it and keep her head up, they were all with her. After this, Jeff could see his young setter slowly start to relax and play with confidence. Each error was met with a shower of reassurances from her teammates. Caroline led her team to victory in game two and continued her amazing play in game three as the Bees went on to upset their rivals, giving them what would be their only conference loss that year!

Maybe pounding a garbage can isn't silly after all?

CREATING TEAM UNITY

Anytime a team is faced with a challenge that they must work together to overcome, and they are successful, they develop a greater sense of trust and confidence as a group. When a team confronts and overcomes a series of such challenges, their sense of team trust, unity, and togetherness builds with each success. They are then able to meet and defeat even greater future challenges due to their increased trust and confidence in each other's ability to be successful in difficult situations. A team-wide sense of **together we can do this** develops.

One highly successful method of helping a team develop a sense of unity is to involve them in **Team Challenges.** These are simply group problem solving activities that can be set up either indoors or outdoors. No expensive equipment or elaborate setup is necessary. Any coach in any situation can use them!

The 1996 Asics/VOLLEYBALL NCAA Division III Coach of the Year, Marty Petersen, has been using team challenges with her University of Wisconsin-Oshkosh teams for the past nine seasons with fantastic results. Prior to the start of the 1988 season Coach Petersen came across a program of team-building activities being used by the Blackhawk Council Girl Scout Organization of Madison, Wisconsin. Since implementing these **Team Challenges** she has seen a dramatic improvement in her program's success. In the past nine seasons, the Titans of UW-Oshkosh have finished in the top three in their conference (WWIAC) eight times — including five conference championships. They have also gained eight post-season appearances, including three Final-Four births, finishing second in the nation in 1994.

"Ever since we started our team building activities back in 1988 there has been a remarkable improvement in our team's attitude, my attitude, and our performance. I believe our record speaks for itself. Whether it be a camping trip, ropes course, mental relaxation techniques, activities performed in a gym or classroom, a day trip, a cookout, or whatever activity I can learn and adapt, I believe that creating an environment of Team-Building is extremely important to the success of any team," states Coach Petersen.

The rules of the **Team Challenges** are simple. Groups should have no more than eight players. If your team has more than eight members, split them into two groups. The coach should form the groups so that they don't become cliques. Each challenge should take no more than 20-30 minutes to solve.

IMPORTANT: The coach is not to be involved in the challenge or tell the players how to accomplish a task. Even if a group appears stumped, only small hints should be offered. Remember: the challenge is for the team to accomplish, not the coach.

"TOGETHER WE CAN" CHALLENGES

The following **Team Challenges** can be done by the whole team together as one group:

1. **The Caterpillar:** The challenge is for the group to become a caterpillar and travel from a starting line to an ending boundary to be determined by the coach (20-40 ft.). Each member of the group must become connected and remain as a part of a "group caterpillar" while traveling with a certain number of appendages touching the ground. To figure out how many appendages your caterpillar may have touching the ground, multiply the number of people in the group by 1.5. The resulting number is how many appendages may touch the ground. Half of the appendages must be hands.

   Variations: 1. Subtract two from the number of appendages and try again.

   2. Try going backwards.

146

2. **Team on a Towel:** Lay a towel out flat on the floor. The challenge is that the whole group must stand on the towel for at least ten seconds, without anyone touching the ground around the towel.

   Variation: Fold the towel to make a smaller area.

3. **Walk the Plank:** You will need two (twelve foot long 2 x 6) planks. Lay the planks end to end, lengthwise. Number each player and have them get on the planks in that order. The challenge is that the players have to go to the reverse number's spot without falling off the plank (one goes to the six position, six to the one spot and so on). Set a scoring goal they must stay under — scoring one point against the team each time a player touches the ground.

4. **Navigator:** Mark off an area twenty by forty feet. Call this the "river." Place a player at one end of the river and a blindfolded teammate at the other. The rest of the team "get into" the river and use their bodies to make up rocks, logs, trees, bridges, etc. in the river. The challenge is that the sighted player (navigator) tries to talk the blindfolded teammate through the river without touching any of the "objects." Next, the blindfolded player becomes the navigator and another team member dons the blindfold.

Note: This challenge calls for precise directions and listening skills. Team members serving as objects in the river cannot talk.

Are you ready for more inner game insights? Turn the page and discover what awaits you in "the beyond."

PART FIVE

And Beyond...

"If one advances confidently in the direction of his own dreams, and endeavors to live the life he has imagined, he will meet with success unexpected in common hours."

Henry David Thoreau

Chapter Eighteen

MORE INNER GAME STUFF

"The golden opportunity you seek is in yourself. It is not in your environment, luck or chance, or from the help of others. It is in yourself, alone."

Orison Swett Marden

YOUR BLUE RIBBON PANEL OF TOP COACHES

As an athlete, how would you like to be able to consult with Al Scates, Terry Liskevych, John Kessel, Bill Neville, Debbie Brown, Jim Stone or any other top coach you respect before a match? Better yet, if you're a coach, how about being able to listen to their advice while devising a match strategy or solving a coaching problem? You can!

Within your mind, there is an infinite storehouse of ideas, know-how, and untapped power. Ralph Waldo Emerson said, "There is one mind common to all individuals." He was talking about the ocean of the universal mind whose inlets reach out to the minds of all people. Many great inventors, writers, composers, and philosophers believe their creations came from a source outside themselves.

All of us have access to this universal mind as we have access to the endless amount of information, facts, and ideas that we've stored in our memory banks. Data accumulated from attending camps, reading books and magazines articles, and sharing ideas with fellow athletes and coaches has been permanently recorded in our brain. We also have a capacity for acquiring knowledge that transcends the sensory experience. In fact, we all have an extrasensory capacity, a creative ability to remember a thought that we never knew before!

151

You don't believe it? Have you ever had a creative idea, an inspiration, a sudden revelation or intuition that solved a stubborn problem? Sure you have. The creative thoughts in this book are proof that we have tapped a greater power. Stan often wonders how he accessed certain thoughts. This same creative process is available to all of us all the time. We have only to learn how to tap the creative process of our subconscious to get answers to life's problems and challenges.

What does it take to access this magical process? Nothing more than clearly identifying the problem as one that is important for you to solve and presenting it to your subconscious mind before falling asleep at night. Then all it takes is being smart enough in the morning to trust the hunch your subconscious produced while you were sleeping. Sounds easy enough.

THE SLEEP-ON-IT TECHNIQUE

Let's say you're a coach who wants to develop a game plan for a big rival match coming up. You're worried because you're uncertain how to defend their middle attack. Should you double block and try to cover the off speed shots to the open area, or single block, and try to dig their awesome middle hitter's spikes? You're unsure about a couple of other things. Especially bothering you are your front row matchups and what will be your best lineup, a problem you've been struggling with all season. Every five minutes you change your mind. Fearful you'll make the wrong decision, you find yourself rethinking it again and again. Your overconcern is making it more difficult to come up with a solid match plan you have confidence in.

Try our **"Sleep On It" technique.** Before going to sleep silently present the problem to your mighty subconscious. While relaxed and lying in bed ask your trusty subconscious to solve the specific problem you're wrestling with. Relaxation is essential since it opens a direct avenue to your subconscious. Apply the same breathing technique we recommend athletes use to relax before visualizing a weak skill into a strength (refer to page 60 to review).

Now do this: With your eyes closed visualize yourself sitting at a large conference table. Imagine sitting at your side are the nationally known coaches mentioned at the start of this chapter (all of whom you hold in high regard). These coaches are there for only one purpose...to determine the best strategy plan for your next match. In detail present all of the scouting facts and figures you have on your opponent's tendencies to this committee of experts. Include an explanation (keep it as objective as you can) of your own team's strengths and weaknesses. The more complete you make the scouting report for both teams the better. Now present the various options you have. Expect no immediate answers. You'll have the right one upon awakening in the morning.

During sleep your subconscious mind takes over and determines the best strategy for you to take. The creative power of your success mechanism scans the mentally stored facts that you have provided. Then it selects the pertinent data, ties it all together (perhaps filling in some vacant spots by tapping a few ideas from the Board of Experts) and reliably serves you the answer in the form of a hunch the next morning. Upon awakening you must totally trust and decisively act upon the revelation you have just received.

Stan has used this same method for finding the best solutions for his coaching problems as well as for writing his books. When words on his word processor are not flowing, at night he creates a board of successful writers, coaches, and sports psychologists whose work he admires. He asks them for creative help after presenting them with the chapter outline he's working on. The first time he used the **"Sleep On It"** technique Stan could not believe the incredible state of concentration and creativity he experienced that next day.

You can call it luck or coincidence. Explain it any way you want. There have been too many **"Sleep On It"** success stories not to believe in its merits. Why don't you judge for yourself? Give it a sincere effort and become a believer in the power that lies within and the power that lies beyond!

POST GAME ANALYSIS: REFRAME AND LET GO

After a match both athletes and coaches should make it a habit not to dwell on the mistakes for too long. Briefly evaluate what went wrong and before you consciously dismiss the emotional debris of the mistakes from your mind, reframe the mistakes into a valuable learning experience. Do you remember the three reframing steps?

1. See a star player finish the same play you didn't. Was it a spike that went awry, a missed serve, or a shanked pass? Imagine the best player on your team executing that same skill you misplayed.

2. Jump inside the winner and feel yourself redo the action. Make it an "inside-out" experience and in slow motion.

3. Abandon the star. Now it's you again with an identical game opportunity. This time feel yourself mastering the action with a successful finish.

This applies to athletes and coaches. After a match, emotions are usually still too high to make judgments on yourself or your teammates. You don't want to entertain any detailed analysis after a loss. Stop punishing yourself and others. If you're a coach, don't make the big mistake of righting the wrongs immediately after a match. Support your players. Quickly clear the residue of pain from the locker room air by expressing hopeful and optimistic terms such as: "Forget it!" "Put it behind you!" "Clear!" "Let-go!" or the great line from the novel, *Gone With The Wind*, "Tomorrow's another day." As depressed and even overwhelmed as you and your players might feel after a defeat, there is a fact that you all should realize...**tomorrow is another day.**

Don't be guilty of critiquing a match to death in the locker room after a loss. If you're a coach who lists match objectives on a chalkboard before a match, we see no problem in having your team with a show of hands vote on whether the written objectives were achieved. But go no further. Tomorrow is another day. Analysis rhymes with paralysis. Overthinking rhymes with overstinking. Incidentally, make certain that the first practice after a tough loss isn't a workout of drudgery and punishment. Make it as much fun as you can. Have players switch positions or perhaps have the last two players on the bench choose teams for drill competition and scrimmages. They'll appreciate it and so will you afterwards.

Your Opponents Have Success mechanisms, Too

One year Dave had a very successful team until they were knocked out in the first round of the post season tournament by a team they had soundly beaten twice that year. Was it overconfidence? Maybe. Was it an accident? No way!! Dave's opponents played his Wildcats evenly throughout the match and pulled off the upset by scoring the last five points of game three for a 16-14 victory. Dave remembers that his opponents appeared to play with a greater sense of purpose and desire to win. Cybernetically speaking, unbeknownst to Dave's Wildcats, their playoff opposition had already set their success mechanisms for optimal performance in practice with a **"whatever it takes"** attitude.

There were warnings that things would not go right for his Wildcats. Dave recalls at the time that he felt his team was ready to be beaten. In the week leading up to the match the practices had gone poorly. The Wildcats were listless, going through the motions — practicing without emotion. Dave could see he was not getting the needed leadership from his seniors either. Sensing the problem worsening, Dave spoke to one of his captains a few days prior to the match, "It's like we're in gridlock, Coach," she admitted. "I don't know what's wrong but we'll be OK," he was assured. However, their less than excited body language, facial expressions, and talk prior to the match gave Dave another impression. Everything he observed was making him insecure about the outcome of the upcoming match. Cybernetically speaking, everything that was happening to his team was contributing to a partially "plugged up" success mechanism.

To no avail Dave tried to remind his team that the team on the other side of the net also had success mechanisms inside their heads. It was too late. As it turned out, their proud opponents were determined not to experience the pain of being beaten a third time by the Wildcats. Their subconscious was set to produce the game of their lives.

Dave remembers the feeling that developed after he took time to "reframe" his own frustration and disappointment into a valuable learning experience over the season's unexpectedly early end. It was the same feeling of appreciation and respect of a job well done that he usually had toward his own team after one of their big wins, except this time it was directed toward his valiant opponents. A less talented team with greater urgency and commitment had beaten his team. Did the best team win? That is not relevant. What's valid is that a less talented team obviously communicated a stronger, more powerful reason to their subconscious. Then they went out on the floor and paid the price success requires.

Why? Was it a state of mind of "wanting to win" the match more than Dave's Wildcats? Whatever the reason, there remains a lesson here to remember as long as you play volleyball. **You are not the only one on the court with a success mechanism! Respect your opponents' right to activate theirs!**

Winners Never Stop Setting Goals

For the senior who has played his or her last game and there is no tomorrow's match or practice, there is a natural letdown. Reaching the end of the season for a graduating athlete means the end of a high school career. Coaches also feel the heaviness of the season's end. Only when players and coaches become involved in setting new goals for projects ahead is there a feeling of excitement once again. New goals bring a renewed sense of energy and enthusiasm. Real happiness comes from the work in striving towards a goal, not in achieving it. Never stop setting goals no matter what, and your subconscious will always cooperate.

How To Program Better Grades And Higher College Board Scores

Why stop at programming just volleyball skills and attitudes into your mental computer? You can select and obtain academic goals, too. Obviously, achievement in the classroom is important in itself, but poor work habits and attitudes in school work often carry over as poor work habits and attitudes on the court. A student-athlete who is irresponsible in the classroom is usually unreliable on the court. This is especially true when conditions are threatening. The athlete reverts to her old thinking and performing habits. When challenged in the gym, the athlete who is unmotivated and failing in school applies the same comfort zone effort she uses in the classroom.

"I just don't like school," (which means I don't like to work in school) in the gym becomes "Aggressiveness isn't my thing." "I'm not smart enough" converts to "I'm not good enough" in the gym. Classroom values such as laziness, forgetfulness, procrastination, projection, rationalization, and disinterest spill over onto the volleyball floor. Underachieving students easily become permanent losers in the gym by applying these same negative classroom habits of thinking and doing. Short range daily goals aren't met, assignments are late, chapters aren't read, projects are seldom completed, and preparation for exams is minimal. Performance on the court can be similarly unacceptable, especially when the challenge is threatening.

A common reason for a negative attitude is fear of failure. Fear controls your expectations — in turn controlling your destiny in the classroom and in the gym. Of course, at the source of the problem is an inadequate self-image. (Where have you heard that before?) It's important to set realistic, achievable, short range goals that provide the underachieving student athlete with a series of small wins. Coupled with constant self-reinforcement through repetitive visualization, modeling, and positive self talk, the athlete's self-image and comfort zone both grow.

Are you an underachiever in the classroom or on tests including college entrance exams? Here are the **Cybernetic** techniques to guide you towards a more fulfilling destiny in school and subsequently in the gym:

1. **Goal Card.** Write an exact numerical grade you want on a goal card for each one of your subjects or for a test you are about to take. For example: 85 on a test or in a course or a qualifying score on your boards. Duplicate the card so that it can be placed in several places — in your wallet, on your desk, or the inside cover of your course notebook.

2. **Time Limit.** Establish a deadline by which you will attain this grade or achieve this test score. Write the time line on your goal card. Will it come on the next unit test, chapter, or report? The more immediate, the better.

3. **Sign the Card.** Sign the card and put the words *"I CAN"* on the top line. Place the card where you can see it conveniently.

4. **Visualize the Grade.** Program your subconscious for achievement with the power of visualization. Awaiting sleep or upon awakening while lying in bed are excellent opportunities to program yourself. Before you begin your visualization session, take a moment and think about what you'll gain should your grade or test score increase. Also think about what you'll lose if you don't increase your scores. This will provide the leverage you'll need to do what we are about to ask you. Visualize the following scene on a large imagined screen.

Mentally picture the academic goal you desire. Visualize it as an accomplished fact. Vividly see yourself on this screen receiving the specified grade, handing in the project, reading the assignment, or passing the College Board tests with the scores that you need. Experience that good feeling of achievement. In the movie, see your friends, coaches, or parents congratulating you on a job well done. Stay with this movie as long as you can. Don't forget to actually picture the grade or goal you need to obtain. Flash it on and off like a neon sign.

Now, take one step backwards in time. See yourself walking into the classroom about to take the test. Notice how confident you are as you walk in and sit down. You're sitting exactly like the smartest student in the room is sitting. Your facial expression and body language are identical to your super smart role model. Take another step backwards in time. In your mind envision yourself working on the assignment or preparing for your College Board test. You are enthused, hard-working, and enjoying the work. Your work ethic is the same as your smart model. Envision yourself enjoying the academic challenge as she or he does. Hold this movie as long as you can in your imagination until you feel the confidence growing inside. Repeat the movie several times. Let it become more real, vivid, and detailed each time you run it.

5. **Act As If.** As you're taking the test think of yourself as that good student you modeled in your visualization exercise. Remember to walk into the classroom as if you are this person. Sit up the way he or she sits when taking a test. Talk to yourself the way you think he or she would while taking a test. Move, look, and feel as if you are this person. Give your best effort preparing for the test, visualizing the best result. Then, relax and let it happen. Replicate the bright student's body language, self-talk, and strategy, and just do it. Don't waste a second worrying about the results. If you can't achieve this relaxed state of mind, that's okay. Just act as if you can.

This method has helped many struggling athletes achieve higher scores on tests. We know it can work for you if you give it your best. We are not suggesting that you substitute this programming process in place of hard work and study, but use it along with them.

The captain of the ship is the master of her fate as long as she keeps her destination in mind. Like that captain, you'll need to keep a clear picture of your final destination in mind. Don't be discouraged whenever an academic goal isn't attained immediately. Anything that is worthwhile takes time. A plane flying from New York to Los Angeles is off course 90% of the time, yet it still gets there. The plane's cybernetic directional system is programmed to land at Los Angeles International Airport.

Setting your subconscious for a correct landing in the classroom means staying with your flight plan and your academic programming process as well. **One step short of success is failure.** So keep stepping in the direction of your scholastic goals no matter what happens enroute. Arrival time may not be when you want, but you'll get there if you remain persistent.

Chapter Nineteen

YOU'VE GOT TO LOVE IT

"When love and skill work together, expect a miracle."
John Ruskin

LOVING THE BALL

There are two essential ingredients necessary for a successful volleyball journey. They are the ball and your dream. If you seriously expect the best from yourself, you'll need both. The dream, without daily exposure to the ball, will never transcend beyond the fanciful daydream stage. The ball, without exposure to your dream, will remain nothing more than a fun object of play. Combine both and a life of exploration, adventure, and growth awaits you. Love both unconditionally and chances are self-fulfillment also awaits. The sooner you build a feeling of love, sacrifice, and commitment with the ball and your dream, the sooner you'll enjoy the benefits of the relationship.

Obviously, you love your dream to some degree or else you wouldn't have progressed this far into this book. We must ask, "Do you love, sincerely love, the ball with the same passion?" Loving the ball is an absolute must. A wonderful definition of love is **looking for good.** Do you see the best qualities in your volleyball as you pick it up and stare at it or do you see frustration, anger, disappointment, and betrayal.

Eric Segal wrote in his book *Love Story,* **"Love means never having to say you're sorry."** Do you enjoy a forgiving relationship with your ball? You ought to, because you can bet the great volleyball players do. Observe the way the "great ones" pick up a volleyball and you'll see a magical rapport that goes beyond respect. Look carefully and you'll find a sense of oneness and bonding between these players and their ball.

However, there is a less intense relationship between average players and their ball. At times there is a feeling of closeness similar to the love that exists between the great players and their ball, but on this less consistent lower level of performance, the relationship is more fickle. Should the ball act deviously for just a crucial moment in a game, the relationship quickly cools. There are good days and bad for them and their ball. Maybe it's because the average player's love is too conditional and based on immediate gratification.

For the poor performing player, the ball-player relationship is tenuous at best. Unfortunately, their association has been built on the negative feelings of disdain, distrust, disrespect, and aversion. Their relationship is so painful, you don't even want to be on the same team with them. In fact their relationship generates so much tension, it affects the relationship between you and the ball.

Fixing the blame as to who's at fault is not the issue. Fixing the relationship is. May we offer you some ball-you-dream counseling advice? You will have to be the strong one and change. Don't expect the ball to meet you halfway. If things can't be worked out, the ball will have no trouble "moving on" and finding someone else who will take better care of it. Hopefully, you'll listen to our advice with an open head and heart. The relationship and what it offers surely is worth saving. May we suggest that you learn how to better love the ball? There...it's been said and we're not ashamed we said it.

HOW TO LOVE THE BALL

We counsel you to:

1. Spend more quality and quantity time alone with your ball. You cannot talk love. You have to live it. When you are not passing, setting, or serving it, keep it close at hand when you're off the court. Put it on your lap while you're watching TV. Put it on your bed at night and sleep next to it. Enjoy its company. Notice when you awake in the morning that it's always there within reach. Before you pick it up, stare at it. Isn't it a magnificent, perfect, and an attractive companion? Now, pick it up in your hands and feel its smooth, soft, expensive white leather coat. A perfect design, too.

2. Your "best pal" loves to be passed, especially by your strong but caring forearms. Because of leathery resiliency, the ball won't damage easily. It can take a blow. Ask it what it likes and it will tell you it enjoys the soft, quick set the best. So set it often on and off the court. For variation try doing tricks with it. It loves creativity. Bounce it off all kinds of surfaces. Once it understands what you expect from it notice how consistently it obeys your commands. Imagine that there is a string attached from the ball to your hands, and no matter how fast it travels, your hands manage to reach it, sending it dutifully to a destination of your choice. Because of the care you are showing the ball, it equally loves you in return and wants nothing better than to please you.

3. To further increase your sensitivity with your ball close your eyes when setting. If the ball occasionally eludes you, don't show anger or disappointment. The ball is your companion and should occasionally be allowed to express its own personality. Its shape is perfect but

159

its personality isn't. Is yours? After an occasional erratic response communicate with the ball by continuing to quietly set it, until you and your ball are in synch once again. This may take some time, so be patient. The relationship will endure if you will just trust one another during times of trial.

4. The ball loves to travel by air. Reward its trustworthiness with countless flights. Start each day with casual sets above your head while lying in bed, sitting in a chair, or standing. On each soft set allow the ball to gracefully leave your hand, making sure it touches your index fingers and thumbs last. The familiarity and trust you develop with these intimate setting sessions will pay remarkable dividends when you get on the court.

5. You are now one with your ball. The two of you are bonded into a single entity. Two spirits — one body. Find a court and start serving your ball. Don't make a conscious effort to serve it in. Let the ball take any arc and destination it wants. Allow your serving action to become a **"let it happen"** swing. Easy does it. No unnecessary rushing. You're not forcing the serve. You're serving the ball simply because it is there to be served. Consider it nothing more than an opportunity to develop a trusting relationship. With time and the total acceptance of the missed serves, you will be pleased to discover how accurate your serve has become. You must understand that real lasting relationships are never based on good times alone but on how well the bad times are handled. Acceptance is a very helpful and powerful attitude to have in a relationship that is evolving. Think of a missed serve or any playing mistake as an opportunity to prove to the ball that you accept its erratic flight. Are you willing to take full responsibility for the wayward result? If you are, watch what happens. In a short time, there'll be fewer and fewer serves off target.

Now that you have listened to our advice, are you willing to bring a feeling of true kinship involving the volleyball and yourself into one loving family? Stephen Covey writes a simple mission statement for the family which might interest you:

> **"To love each other...**
> **To help each other...**
> **To believe in each other...**
> **To wisely use your time, talents and resources...**
> **Together."**

So what are you waiting for? Have a family meeting right now! Communicate your deepest feelings of affection to your volleyball. It could be the beginning of a very beautiful relationship.

Are we being silly or serious? You decide!

Chapter Twenty

THE REAL VALUE OF YOUR VOLLEYBALL JOURNEY

"Heroes are those who go beyond themselves to make a difference for others."
Raul Julia

Congratulations, you made it this far! Have you gotten the results you wanted? Outcome is important. So is the direction you're heading. Since you're investing all of this time, energy, and pain into the game of volleyball, may we ask you, when your playing days are over how do you want to be remembered? When others reminisce about your playing career, what is it you want them to be saying? Do you want to be remembered as the best role player on the team, someone who consistently contributed to the team's success? Or do you want to be recalled as a tough competitor who did what had to be done to win a game? Or do you want to be thought of as a step-up performer whose game elevated during the closing points of a match?

From the start of this book, we have focused on achieving whatever dream you wanted. But once attained, what then? Another dream perhaps? Now that you are aware of your **Internal Success System** and understand our **FAST** formula for activating it, you can walk into the field of endless possibilities.

What if we told you there is an even more glorious dream of achievement out there? Go for this one and others will be talking about you for a long, long time and in the most glowing terms, too. We're talking about a dream that requires a level of performance that you're more than capable of reaching. Although all athletes have the ability to perform at this lofty height, few do. It's unfortunate since the rewards at this level are bountiful. Before we tell you about this ultimate level of performance and explain what the **"Big One"** is all about, may we play a little game?

Try to imagine that your volleyball destiny is a building — a four story structure. Now picture your subconscious as the elevator and your belief system as the operator capable of taking you to the floor of your choice. Let's take a look at your choices.

On floor one you find athletes who play volleyball for the fun of it. There is nothing wrong with them, except they rarely pick up a volleyball or "pay the price" between seasons. Since the game isn't that important to them, you won't find them diligently working on their playing weaknesses or physical conditioning. Because their habit is to value entertainment over hard work, they're easy to spot on the court. A bored facial expression and pained body language during drills quickly give them away. Frankly, they would rather play than prepare. "When are we going to play?" is their favorite question. Should you decide to get off on this floor, we must warn you, it's crowded here.

On floor two you find players who look for the winning edge. They practice and play hard, but unfortunately their game is saddled with one glaring deficiency. They're afraid they'll "mess it up!" They tie their shoelaces just like any big play performer, but whenever their team needs a huge effort, they play as if their shoelaces are tied together. Fearful of making a mistake, they tend to play too conservatively. Their play is predictable. Risk taking is not a part of their game plan, neither is mastery.

The third floor is for the prime time athletes who work hard and are not afraid to "mess it up." They thrive on competition and never worry about the consequences of taking a chance and failing. A major quality of these athletes on floor three is not their talent alone but their courage and self-trust. They win championships, receive trophies, and earn scholarships mainly because they believe in themselves and love the thrill of the action regardless of the score. Is this the highest level to strive for?... Or reach?

There is another floor above — a fourth floor for those willing to enjoy an even greater reward. Interestingly, athletes who make it to this upper level may not be the most talented or even garner the most playing time. But don't make the mistake of not appreciating their accomplishments or modeling their performance. They are excellent role models who lead by example. Pay close attention to them. They can teach you so much more about the joys of life than any of the highly glorified and publicized winners on the third floor. They are talked about in admiration long after their playing days are over. Let us tell you about these fourth floor residents.

- The decisions they make both on and off the court are guided by a value system that stresses hard work, determination, compassion, optimism, loyalty, unselfishness, caring, courage, trust, and respect.

- Although they may not be the best athletes on the team, you won't find any better role models to follow.

- Because they do and say the right thing at the right time, their greatest quality is they make you feel very good about yourself when you are in their company.

- Those who make it to this floor never set out to lead the field or become the standard bearer of high principles for others to follow. They never consciously seek the spotlight as a leader or hero.

- Glory isn't the name of their game but integrity, humility, and team contribution are.
- They are the kind of athletes not interested in how many sets they get to attack, but rather how well they attack the sets they get. A poor choice by their setter doesn't mean they didn't get set, it means the best option on the play didn't get the ball.
- Regardless of the playing time they receive, you won't ever hear them complain.
- They're the first at practice, the last to leave, and always come ready to work.
- They never learned how to point a finger of blame. When things go wrong, you'll never find them fixing the blame. They major in fixing problems.
- They may not always agree with their coach's strategy, but no one will ever know it. Loyalty is an important quality of their character.
- Never talking about others behind their back is one of their best habits.
- However, they are not shy in telling teammates who habitually break training rules or are performing selfishly to straighten out.
- When teammates commit playing mistakes they are the first to encourage them to hang tough.
- Those who qualify for the fourth floor love the thrill of the challenge. The tougher the practice the more they like it.
- In games they hustle no matter what the score or who the opponent is.
- With an optimistic eye they tend to recognize what went right in practice or a match.
- For them setbacks are temporary and offer good opportunities for learning.
- They never take criticism personally. No pity parties for them. No sulking or self-indulgence either. They let the coach coach.
- Since they are in great shape twelve months a year, they never seem to get sick or miss a practice or match.
- Coaches trust them implicitly and so do their teammates.
- Whenever the coach talks to the team, their eyes are glued on the coach. They are exceptional listeners and learners.
- They observe, study, and remember. We are not talking IQ, but sincerity of purpose and focus.
- They have an inner eye to see the big picture...not what is, but what will be.
- They need no external motivation from their coach or well meaning parents telling them what to do. They are self-assigners.
- Since they know what they want they have no trouble challenging themselves in practice and between seasons.
- In spite of the fact that they are not the biggest, quickest, or the best, they are without a doubt the most determined and resilient.
- They never learned how to quit.

This is the **Big One!** The fourth floor! The highest level you can reach. It's there for the taking, or should we say **for the giving?** You don't have to review this list to know that these athletes are big time givers, not takers. A self-serving, **"What's in it for me?"** is not in their makeup. **"How can I help?"** however, is. Think for a moment about the people who have helped you become who you are. Didn't they possess many of these qualities of character? If you haven't modeled their empowering qualities by now, what's holding you back?

When you do decide to model them, look around. You just might find a parade of others modeling you. It's called the **processional effect.** Unselfish service is contagious and has a habit of multiplying. By doing the right thing it's hard to predict how many others you touch down the line with your giving and caring actions. Could this be the real value of your volleyball journey...to help others? Now you have another reason to go for the **Big One.**

THE EAGLE THAT THOUGHT IT WAS A CHICKEN

Once upon a time there was a chicken farm located at the foot of one of the great Rocky Mountains. It was one of the finest farms in the entire Great Northwest. Much of the credit for the success of the chicken farm was due to the dedication of the farmer who cared for the chickens.

Each evening after dinner, it was the farmer's daily custom to climb the foothill of the mountain that overlooked his farm. As the sun was setting behind him, he would marvel at the beauty of his farm below. One evening standing on a bluff, he heard the hungry cry of a small bird behind him. The farmer turned to find a baby eagle alone in a nest, apparently abandoned and left to die. From the look of the eagle's emaciated body, it had a severely damaged wing and was close to death.

The farmer had a vision. He would nurse the eagle back to health at his farm and then return it to the sky where it belonged. The farmer placed the eagle into one of the open pens with the chickens and began feeding it by hand. With each passing day, the eagle grew bigger and stronger, but never once did it try to fly out of the pen. The farmer noticed the wild creature truly enjoyed being with the domesticated chickens. Eating, playing, and sleeping with the chickens provided the eagle with everything it wanted. For the eagle life appeared full.

Weeks passed into months as the eagle grew to full size. Remembering his promise, the farmer decided it was time to return the wild creature to the sky where it belonged. He was confident that a little jump start was all the eagle needed to fly.

Picking up the eagle, the farmer threw the bird high over his head. The eagle instinctively spread its wings and was about to fly, when it made the mistake of looking down toward the chickens with whom it had spent such a delightful time. Suddenly, the eagle lost altitude, spiraled down toward the chicken pen, and landed with an awkward thud.

The farmer was amused, but determined. Again, picking up the eagle, he climbed a nearby ladder and threw the eagle up as high as he could. The eagle made the same mistake of looking down at the chickens and once again landed with an embarrassing thud in the dust of the chicken pen.

"This bird thinks it's a chicken," the farmer mused. This time, picking up the eagle by the neck (the farmer's frustration beginning to show), he walked over to the ranch house, climbed onto the roof, and proceeded to toss the eagle as high as he could into the air.

From the sheer force of the throw, feathers flew out of the eagle's body. Furiously the eagle flapped its wings and was about to become airborne, when it committed the same mistake of looking down toward the chicken pen. Once again, the eagle belly flopped into the dust of the chicken pen.

"I give up," the farmer exclaimed, "This stupid eagle thinks it is a chicken." And so he did give up trying to get the eagle to fly. This would have been the end of the story had it not been for a passing stranger. Walking by the chicken farm, he came upon the pen in which the eagle lived. Amazed by the sight of this magnificent wild creature living with the chickens, the stranger went to the farmhouse to inquire. The farmer explained the entire course of events: finding the abandoned eagle, nursing it back to health, and not being able to get the eagle to fly. The stranger listened to the story and then said bluntly, "I know I can get the eagle to fly. Please let me try." There was a sense of confidence in the stranger's voice that impressed the farmer. "Be my guest, but I must warn you, that eagle absolutely thinks it is a chicken."

The stranger walked over to the chicken pen in which the eagle was sleeping and with the greatest of care picked up the eagle. Carrying the bird tucked under his arm, the stranger headed toward the mountain and began the perilous journey to its top.

As you can imagine, climbing a mountain is no easy task, especially carrying a full size eagle. Ascending a mountain is akin to the journey of life (or even the journey of a long volleyball season). Along the way, all journeys present challenges. This particular mountain was no exception. There were dangerously narrow paths, rugged rocks, fallen trees, deep rivers, even threatening cliffs. It took the stranger, eagle in hand, all day and all night to struggle to the top of the mountain. At dawn with the sun rising in the east, they finally reached the very top of the mountain.

What a strange sight it was. Silhouetted against the bright orange light of the morning sky stood the stranger holding the eagle in his hands. Staring straight into the confused eyes of the eagle, the stranger commanded in a strong voice, **"Thou art an eagle, spread thy wings and fly. You belong to the heavens!"** Instantly the stranger threw the eagle high over his head, again shouting **"Thou art an eagle, spread thy wings and fly. You belong to the heavens."** As the eagle began to rise into the sky, it repeated the mistake of looking down. But this time the eagle was too high up to see the chickens, the chicken pen, or even the farm.

Then a wonderful thing happened to the eagle. Rising upward, it felt the force of the wind beneath its wings and the rush of the cold mountain air against its face. The eagle began to inspect the magnificent panoramic scene of the cloudless sky and the endless horizon with the rugged beauty of the mountains below. The eagle seemed to suddenly realize the infinite opportunities that free flight offered. An incredible feeling of excitement, power, and freedom flowed through its body. It was unlike any other feeling the eagle had experienced living in the chicken pen.

Then the eagle heard the voice of the stranger crying out one final time, **"Thou art an eagle, spread thy wings and fly. You belong to the heavens."** And for the first time, it understood what the stranger was saying. The eagle finally realized that its destiny was in the sky and it began to fly effortlessly higher and higher. As it was about to disappear into the early morning sky, it dove toward the stranger, dipping its wings as if to say, "Thank you!" Before the stranger realized it, the eagle was gone.

The eagle never returned to the farm, nor did the stranger. There are evenings when the farmer, standing on the bluff and with the wind blowing just right, thinks he hears the joyous cry of a free flying eagle coming from the sky above the mountain.

So ends our favorite story of *The Eagle That Thought It Was A Chicken*. But the end of this story is really the beginning for all of us. Are you ready for the infinite opportunities of flight awaiting you on your volleyball journey? We hope you are. Before getting airborne yourself, you'll have to hurdle the fence of your comfort zone and that means **paying the price** of some discomfort.

We hope you'll trust our **Cybernetic** flight plan. Remember before you can fly, you have to firm up the reason you want to soar. Without a compelling reason, you'll find yourself spiraling downward into the dust of your own comfort zone at the first sight of trouble. Just remember what this book teaches. Any time you meet a challenge on your flight, simply **act as if** you can do whatever has to be done. Think, feel, talk to yourself and fly as if you are an eagle. After all, you are one!

By the way, you can expect to see a lot more chickens than eagles on your personal journey through life. Just remember these two key rules for high flying and you'll be all right:

> **Rule #1: Ignore those chickens.**
> **Rule #2: Pay close attention to the eagles.**

Make it your habit to model the strategies of eagles, only. Hopefully, your journey will be smooth and safe. But don't count on it! Especially while flying high. Do we have to warn you about the unpredictable crosswinds of life? They're there to test your resolve and make you stronger. When hardships happen remind yourself, **"Thou art an eagle, spread thy wings and fly. You belong to the heavens."**

THE FINAL CHOICE IS YOURS

It is clearly up to you to select your volleyball dream and the path you intend to take to achieve it. Whether you take the inner path of **Volleyball Cybernetics** or not, make sure it's your dream you are reaching for and not someone else's.

Your next step is to decide, specifically, what will bring you the most happiness and go to work to make it (**and let it**) happen. If you want a more accurate serve, additional aggressiveness at the net, or the ability to handle frustration better, the results will be in exact proportion to the time and effort you invest in the **FAST Formula for Success** or any other training program you decide to follow. **Volleyball Cybernetics** has never been a get rich quick plan. Getting what you want requires focus, commitment, and persistence.

After you've made your choices and lived your volleyball dream, what then? Life's road is full of twists and turns that will constantly provide you with opportunities for growth and change, if you'll only keep your eyes open for these golden moments. Often the opportunities take the shape of problems, so don't be deceived. The Chinese have it right. Their word for crisis and opportunity are the same.

And remember to live these three qualities of the overachiever every day of your life:

1. Pay close attention to the winners around you and model what you see, hear, and feel.
2. Assign yourself. Don't wait to be told this is what you must do to improve. Motivate yourself by finding a reason why you must immediately take action. Then do it.
3. Develop that feeling of success by using the power of visualization to see what you want...never what you want to avoid.

Simple enough! Pay attention, assign yourself, and visualize.

Got it? Good. Now, **live it!**

A FINAL THOUGHT

We leave you with a simple prayer that Stan learned from a 16 year-old camper in Ohio. Her parents taught it to her to keep her strong and on track during life's tests.

> *"By your own soul, learn to live.*
> *If others thwart you, take no heed.*
> *If others hate you, have no care;*
> *Sing your song, dream your dream,*
> *Hope your hope and pray your prayer."*

We hope, pray, and dream you find the courage, commitment, and faith to sing your own song. Do you know its lyrics and tune? Just listen closely to your heart, and you will hear the melody. Let the unlimited power of your inner resources be the strong voice you'll need. Please trust the inner game plan detailed in this book. It will help you fulfill your greatest responsibility... to become everything you are meant to be.

Before another moment passes, promise us... you'll live an extraordinary life. Why? Because there is no better way to enjoy life's journey.

Volleyball Cybernetics is a "Yes, I Can!" publication.
Parts of *Volleyball Cybernetics* are available on video and audio cassettes.

For Camp and Clinic Information Contact:
Dave Cross, 365 North Abbe Road, Elyria, Ohio 44035
Phone: 440-365-3329   Fax: 440-365-0321
Dave's Toll Free Phone: 1-877-220-5828
E-Mail: dave@yesicansports.com   Web: www.yesicansports.com

For Book, Video, and Audio Information Contact:
Stan Kellner, P.O. Box 134 VB, East Setauket, New York, 11733
Phone: 516-751-3513   Fax: 516-751-3589
E-Mail: stan@yesicansports.com